Remember Me, Rescue Me

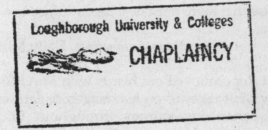

Centre for
Faith and Spirituality
Loughborough University

Remember Me, Rescue Me is a passionate, searing investigation into the evil that men do to the most vulnerable. It focuses on sexploitation of kids in one of the world's richest nations and exposes the suffering of those children, told first hand by so many little voices who for too long have never been heard. If you are concerned about the future of a generation of forgotten children, please read this book. And realise that there must be a better tomorrow for them.

Anton Antonowicz, Daily Mirror

Matt Roper moved our hearts with *Street Girls*. Now Matt takes us on his dangerous, arduous and exhausting journey throughout Brazil, including the Amazon, fact and person-finding into the horrifying jungle of greed, violence, fear, drugs and child abuse.

Remember Me, Rescue Me is well written, fast moving and easily read but also a heart rending, uncomfortable expose which cries for redemption of body, soul and spirit for the thousands of the world's downtrodden and exploited children. Those who follow a redeemer with 'good news for the poor' dare not miss this book.

Roger Forster

Remember Me, Rescue Me

Matt Roper

with David Porter

Authentic
LIFESTYLE

First published in 2003 by Authentic Lifestyle

09 08 07 06 05 04 03   7 6 5 4 3 2 1

Authentic Lifestyle is an imprint of
Authentic Media
PO Box 300, Carlisle, Cumbria, CA3 0QS, UK
and PO Box 1047, Waynesboro, GA 30830-2047, USA
www.paternoster-publishing.com

**A catalogue record for this book is available from the
British Library**

ISBN 1-85078-479-5

Cover design by River
Printed in Great Britain by
Cox and Wyman, Reading, Berkshire, RG1 8EX

Contents

	Acknowledgements	xiii
1	Rio de Janeiro: On Copacabana Beach	1
2	Montes Claros: The Trail Begins	16
3	Jequitinhonha Valley: The Houses of Hopelessness	26
4	Governador Valadares: The One-Ninety-Nine Girls	42
5	Montes Claros Again: The Virgin Auction	63
6	Recife: Summertime Cinderellas	79
7	The Sertão: Impossible Choices	98
8	Fortaleza: 'I'm not a whore, I'm just a little girl'	114
9	Belém: The Bat's Hole	135
10	Santarém: Engraved on the palm of my hands	151
11	Oriximiná: Hell in Paradise Ville	169

12 Manaus: 'Disneylands of Sex'   181
13 Guajará-Mirim: 'Nobody can rescue me
     from this'   197
     Postscript: Islington, London   217
     The Next Chapter: Pedraviva   222

www.mattroper.com

For Daniela

Praise for *Street Girls*

'Accessible…straightforward…so moving.'
Andrew Carey, Celebrate

'Offering insights into lives that you will probably never before have imagined . . . a harrowing and uplifting account of the work of the Meninadança project among the lost girls living on the streets of Brazil.'
Danny Graymore, fish.co.uk

'This is a book that brings stories of hope from desperate situations.'
Lifestyle *Magazine*

'Matt's story is an amazing one… Society has given up on the street girls but not Matt Roper.'
Mary Solarski, Evangelicals Now

'If you don't want to feel challenged, then don't read this book.'

Jean Chalmers

'Disturbing, inspiring, challenging.'

New Directions *Magazine*

'Not since *Chasing the Dragon* by Jackie Pullinger have I been so challenged to abandon all for the kingdom. This is a must read for all who have a heart to be used by God.'

Rex Burgher

'Matt Roper is a visionary with a moving story to tell. If you have ever thought, prayed or merely wished for a Christian response to child abuse you should read what Matt has to say.'

Viv Thomas, author of Future Leader

'Street Girls do not represent an isolated problem but an international concern. Here at last comes a book that introduces us to the reality of the problem... Eye-opening and uncomfortable reading... it also brings a note of anticipation and optimism. There is still hope, at least where Christians are prepared to get involved and take action.'

Clive Calver, World Relief

'An amazing story of such courage and faith, it should be an inspiration to us all. Matt Roper gives us the truth about the lives of the street girls...it has you crying in desperation but also at times from happiness and relief at their successes.'

Living Stones Bookshop website

'As soon as I started reading it I couldn't put it down. I was deeply moved by the terrible yet so amazing stories of the girls in Brazil. The book was so well-written that by the end I really felt that I knew the girls personally.'

Hannah Lock

ACKNOWLEDGEMENTS

My journey around Brazil was funded by Jubilee Action, a human rights charity dedicated to protecting children at risk around the world. For more details visit *www.jubileeaction.co.uk*.

I cannot possibly list all the Brazilians who helped me during my trip, but I especially want to thank:

In Montes Claros: Luiz Ribeiro (*Estado de Minas* newspaper), Egidevaldo Gomes Brito (Juvenile Court); in the Jequitinhonha Valley: Prof. Nebson Escolástico da Paixão (Unimontes); in Governador Valadares: Abigail Gonçalves Silva Correa (Children's Council); in Recife: Roland and Rosa Meylan (Salvation Army), Julie Gali (YWAM); in the Sertão: Márcia Maria Leite de Araújo (Children's Council), Cristiano Jerônimo (*Diário de Pernambuco* newspaper); in Fortaleza: Luizianne Lins (city councillor), Peter and

Selma Thomas (YWAM); in Belem: Marcel Theodor Hazeu (Movimento Emaús); in Santarém: Jeff and Becky Hrubik (PAZ Mission), Br. Ronald David Hein (Pastoral Service), Bernadette de Lourdes Silva Martins (Pastoral Service); in Oriximiná: Mirian Amaral Vinhote (Pastoral Service), Raimundo Cézar da Silva Brito, Edra Simone Amaral Vinhote, Larissa Vinhote Brito; in Manaus: Pablo and Coleen Fast (PAZ Mission); in Guajará-Mirim: Amaury Ribeiro Júnior (*Isto É* magazine), Leopoldo Silva (*Isto É* magazine), Izabel Costa Hayden (Children's Council). A special obrigado to Orlindo Perreira de Souza from Belo Horizonte who gave up four months of his time to help me.

Interviews were always conducted with a second person present. In some places names have been changed to protect them.

My thanks go to Rafael Guimarães from Holy Design in Belo Horizonte (www.holydesign.com.br) for providing the map illustrations and for designing my website.

In the UK, special thanks to my pastor Graham Knott, and to Ted Steiner and the rest of my support group.

Many thanks to David Porter, whose contribution to this book was invaluable. When I began my postgraduate studies I had written the first draft but found myself with very little time to prepare the manuscript for publication. David worked extensively on the text with me over several months, revising and restructuring the narrative throughout and co-writing in some places. I seriously doubt the book would have been written without him. I also learned so much from his experience and skill, and I very much enjoyed our heated arguments about words!

Rio de Janeiro : On Copacabana Beach

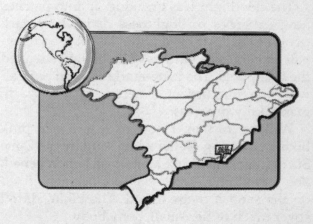

A cool twilight breeze was coming in from the sea as I walked barefoot on the floodlit sands. The blare of music and laughter from the crowded clubs and bars on the promenade began to fade behind me. Far-off waves crashed and rolled in a black invisible sea.

Copacabana Beach was almost deserted. Only strollers like me and a few volleyball players were still on the beach.

I began to walk towards the water line. It was a typical warm, lazy Copacabana evening, the kind that tourists came from all over Brazil and beyond to enjoy. It was the last time I would be able to take such a stroll before returning home to England. Copacabana was one place in crowded Rio where you could be alone.

The floodlight was breaking up into patches now, expanses of brightness divided by dark pools of shadow. Beyond the last of the volleyball players, pale patches of moonlight streaked the tide-pools. The zone-markers, each painted with the number of a sector of the beach, marked my progress.

Walking further, I noticed a girl in a pink bikini, cowering on the white sand by the Zone Six marker. She didn't look up as I approached. She was sitting, knees clasped, her gaze fixed on the sand a metre ahead. The bikini didn't cover much of her small, bony body.

She was about ten years old.

My eyes adjusted to the shadows. A man was standing a few metres behind her, arms folded, guarding her impassively. His eyes flickered menacingly in my direction. I shivered. There could only be one reason for a ten-year-old girl to be on an isolated part of the beach at this time of night. And she was much too valuable for her pimp to allow her to work alone.

Girls like her were the reason I was in Brazil. I had first arrived here five years ago, after reading about the plight of the country's street children while studying for a Music and Media degree back in England. The more time passed, the more convinced I became that I should go – and I felt a growing sense of urgency. No sooner had I graduated than I got on a plane heading for Brazil, determined to do something – although not knowing exactly what. I eventually found myself in an obscure town in the middle of the Amazon jungle, wondering what on earth I had done.

I survived, and six months later I moved on, to Brazil's third largest city and state capital, Belo Horizonte. I began working with the city's street girls, later starting a project called Meninadança, literally 'Girldance'. It offered dance as an alternative high, a way of putting colour and joy back into the girls' lives without the need for the crack-cocaine that was destroying them. We were privileged to see many girls healed and restored, many returning to live with their families. Five years later, the project had helped over two hundred homeless young girls.

More than sixty had left the streets for good.[1]

At Meninadança we worked mainly with young addicts, although each one had her own heartbreaking story to tell of violence and abuse. Prostitution was part of the landscape too. It was one of the ways that the girls fuelled their addictions. Whenever I heard that a girl was selling her body, it tore me up inside.

Some pimps dress their girls up, slashing their thin lips with scarlet, perming their hair and making their lashes black and thickly curled. The girls sway on high heels and pout as they have been taught, trying to charm the passers-by for whom they've become part of the scenery.

The girl on the beach was of the other kind. Most of the very young ones are like her. She wore no make-up; her hair was tied back, exposing a child's face. She was sitting hunched up, not trying to display her body. At ten there was nothing to display, if it was a cheap woman you were looking for. But people who bought girls like this weren't looking for women.

She avoided meeting my eyes.

'What are you doing?' I asked gently.

---

[1] My book *Street Girls: Hope on the Streets of Brazil* (Paternoster Lifestyle, 2001), tells the story of Meninadança.

She didn't answer. She unclasped her hands and became absorbed in tracing a complicated scribble on the sand.

'What's your name?'

No answer. Her finger was making circles, over and over. She was a frightened little girl; she'd needed no lessons in looking vulnerable and scared.

Eventually she looked at me. She seemed very frightened, and occasionally glanced behind her. The man was eyeing me, and getting very agitated. He was large, burly, dark-skinned and stubble-faced; he was wearing trousers and a scruffy shirt. As I tried to get the girl to talk he became increasingly restless. Finally he got to his feet.

The girl tensed, and clasped her knees again, her expression hunted and drawn. I began to feel worried. As he sauntered towards us, I decided to move on.

At the promenade I put my shoes on and looked back. The pimp and his young charge were invisible in the darkness. It was a different world up here: full of neon lights and flashing signs, music blaring through open doors, crowds gathered round outdoor bars and sitting at tables full of bottles and glasses. I made my way to the highway, a double lane of traffic roaring between the famous beach and the seafront hotels. Soon I was safely back in my room.

I kicked off my shoes, scrubbed the white sand from my feet with a threadbare hotel towel, lay on the narrow bed and tried to sleep.

But sleep would not come. As much as I tried, I could not forget that little girl in her pink bikini. She was at the same time like all the other girls I had met in Brazil, and yet different.

She was certainly not unique. I knew little about Brazil's child prostitution industry, but I knew that on Rio's beaches that night other girls were waiting on the darkening sands, their pimps watchful in the shadows.

Maybe she had been taught not to flaunt herself, how to remain a shy, vulnerable child in the client's eyes, even though inside she was already worldly-wise. Her clients were looking for a child. And children did not come cheap. I knew that on Copacabana prices were steep. To pay for a girl like this, and take her back up the beach to a grubby hostel where you could use her, would cost at least 20 *reals*. That was serious money on the beach. For that kind of cash, up on the promenade you could have bought a few beers.

Maybe she seemed different because she was not like the girls who hung round the streets, openly available, waiting for a car to pull up, a man to beckon. If you wanted this child, you had consciously to leave the loud promenade behind you and plunge into the darkness, until you found your ten-year-old for hire.

The evil of the system had shocked me on my arrival in Brazil and it shocked me just as deeply years later. I would never get used to it, never walk down a Brazilian street and not feel heartache for the young lives being broken there.

My brain was storing impressions to go with the photographs and notebooks full of jottings that I had been using to write *Street Girls*, the story of my Brazil experiences. Maybe there was something about the child on the beach that reminded me of other ten-year-olds I knew back in peaceful England – still children, still innocent, still enjoying everything that had been robbed from this little girl in Brazil.

My mind was full of questions. Who was she? What was she doing right now? Was she safe?

After ten minutes I decided to go back and find her. I got out of bed and hurriedly threw on my clothes. I didn't know what I was going to do when I got there, but I went anyway, negotiating the highway traffic and the club crowds on the promenade. The beach was still floodlit – it was early by Copacabana standards – and I easily found my way back to Zone Six. The girl and her pimp had gone.

As I walked back to the hotel I was deep in thought. This girl was not just an individual:

she represented something. Child prostitution was a horror I had been aware of ever since I had arrived in Brazil, but being so involved with the street girls project I had not thought at length about the larger dimensions of the country's child prostitution industry. But I was thinking hard now. How did it come about that such a trade could flourish in one of the world's great nations – a trade that defeated the attempts of the government and international charities to protect its victims and punish those who made money from it? Where was the real power behind the trade in young children? What was really going on?

It was a chain of thought that was to have far-reaching consequences for me. I had no idea then that that encounter on the beach would affect me so deeply. Over the next few months I would think of little else: it would rock my faith and strip it to the core. And then I would embark on a journey that would change my life for ever.

Street Girls was written on a laptop computer before I left Brazil, often in the early hours, wherever I could find space and time to set up my makeshift office. When it was finished I sent the manuscript to England and started to pack.

I had done what I came to Brazil to do. As the plane left the runway and the modern cityscape below gave way to green-topped mountains, the scrubland beyond and eventually the oceans, it felt as if I was leaving part of me behind.

Back in England I needed to plan for the future. I considered various possibilities and decided to apply to City University in London for a postgraduate course in newspaper journalism. It seemed a good way of keeping my options open.

Publication day arrived, and the postman delivered a parcel containing several crisp copies of *Street Girls*. The next day, I went to City University for my interview.

I was offered a place for the next academic year. But I didn't have much time to prepare. *Street Girls* was attracting a great deal of interest. I was invited to speak about my work in Brazil at church services, public meetings and national conferences. I received hundreds of letters and emails from all over the world. A Japanese woman sent an e-mail at 2 am., to tell me she had just finished reading the book and couldn't sleep. Many girls of between fourteen and sixteen years old, the same age as most of the girls in the book, wrote to tell me they had cried their way through it. Many others said that the stories of these young girls had changed their lives. Wesley Owen Books and Word Publishing both made *Street Girls* their book of the month.

However, I had to do something with the rest of my life. I knew that I wanted to write more about Brazil. Although I knew I would never forget the girls we had helped – Pâmela, Poliana, Sofia, and all the others whose lives had touched my own – I knew I had to move on. I had no clear idea what I was going to write, but I knew that sooner or later I would be writing again.

The journalism course was my investment in the future. I had been passionate about human rights even before I went to Brazil: if I was going to spend my life fighting for human rights, I wanted my brain and my technical skills to be as well trained as possible.

Registration day arrived. I sat in the Great Hall at City University with other new students, waiting for my turn to sign forms, answer questions and be formally enrolled.

There were about seventy or eighty of us, all chatting, reading, listening to walkmans or otherwise killing time as the queue slowly moved forward. As each student completed the process and was sent on his or her way, we all picked up our chairs and shuffled one place higher in the queue. It was an exceptionally tedious way of spending a morning.

I exchanged a few words with those sitting nearby but my mind was in Brazil. I was thinking, as I so often had since my return to England, about the people I knew: in the big cities, in the remote towns and villages, in the rainforests. And the girls themselves, so vulnerable yet hard as nails, growing cynical and weary as the drugs enslaved them; many turning to prostitution to feed their habit.

Sometimes you make more progress when you are away from a situation than when you are deeply involved in it. Certainly my perspective on the street girls' plight had broadened as I reflected on all I had learned and as I contemplated becoming a trained journalist. Investigative journalism was what I wanted most to do. I'd often admired people who exposed cover-ups, challenged hypocrisy and used their writing to challenge social injustice. There was a story to be told about Brazil, I recognised, and it was a story I'd been too busy to adequately investigate when I was working at the project. Now it was a story I was burning to tell.

A student walked past, heading for the door. We all picked up our chairs and moved forward. I was only a few places away from the interview desk now; my long wait was coming to an end. I could even hear the droning voices of the University administrators at the admissions desk.

But how could I fight injustice in Brazil? I had thought and prayed long about it. Somehow, sitting in the Great Hall, I was able to see the answer with greater clarity than ever. You fight injustice by exposing it. The Bible talks often about shining light on evil, about exposing the deeds of darkness to the light of day, about the things that belong to the night and are ashamed of the dawn and the coming of daytime.

Another student completed his registration, and we moved forward again with a loud protest of scraping chairs and shuffling feet. My mind was racing.

Were paper qualifications essential for the task? I knew there was a lot I could learn from the course, things I needed to know and skills I would have to have. But did I need all that right now?

As I thought about it, everything fell sharply into focus. I should go back to Brazil and investigate the child prostitution industry, following up the contacts I'd made and the people I needed to talk to. The people who were horrified at what was going on, and who were working to stop it; and the people who were doing very well out of it, thank you, and were very happy to let it continue. I needed to talk to both. And I needed to do it as soon as possible.

There was only one student ahead of me in the queue now. The interview at the admissions desk was coming to an end. The student ahead of me got up ready to take his place at the desk. I stood up, picked up my things and made for the door.

Rio International Airport was as crowded as ever, and sweltering. I collected my bags from

the carousel and trundled my trolley through
the arrivals gate.

'Hey mate, welcome to Rio!'

A man erupted from the crowd. He seized
my bags. 'It's really good to *see* you. How *are*
you?'

I tried to remember who this man was and
why he knew me so well. It was like meeting a
long-lost friend. I couldn't remember telling
anyone I would be arriving.

'Good flight was it? You look tired…'

'Yes … thanks.' I was racking my brains. I
was sure I had seen this man before; I just
couldn't remember where.

'So, where you going?'

'Er … to find a hotel for the night?' I was
completely baffled.

'Well, let's go then!'

He led the way to a lift to the car park, where
he started loading my bags into a brown Ford
Escort. As we passed through the ticket booth
and along a slip-road onto the motorway, I put
my pride in my pocket and asked him who he
was.

'*Me*? I'm the taxi driver!' he beamed.

I gasped. 'So how much is this costing me?'

'Oh, 50 *reals* should do it.'

He put his foot down and swung alarmingly
into the stream of highway traffic heading for
the city. He wove between cars at breakneck
speed, gesticulating to other drivers. My seat

belt did not work, so I gripped onto my seat for
dear life. He turned round and saw the look of
sheer horror on my face.

'Don't worry,' he smiled. 'Rio drivers don't
crash very often, you know.'

'No?'

'No... but when we do crash, we die. Just like
Ayrton Senna.'

Very reassuring, I told him.

'So where you from?'

'England.'

'Hooligans,' he said.

'Eh?'

'Lots of hooligans there, aren't there?'

'Well...'

'So what you doing here?'

'I'm writing a b–'

'Bin Laden,' he interrupted.

'Well no, a *book*.'

'No, that's who you're fighting, aren't you?
Osama?'

'Well, not me *personally*.'

Our bizarre conversation moved from poli-
tics to Princess Diana to the Rolling Stones to
Dolly the Sheep. He talked on enthusiastically,
and I sat back in my seat, suddenly weary after
the long flight. As we careered into Rio's South
Zone, the taxi driver was already onto the more
important subjects – football and women.

'I think English women are too fat. American
women are too ugly. French women smell. And

German women don't shave their armpits!
Yuck!'

As we finally neared my hotel, he had safely
concluded that Brazil has the world's most
beautiful women and the best football team. He
also bet me my taxi fare that Argentina would
knock England out of the World Cup in the first
round. I told him I would be back to collect my
winnings.

Outside, the lights of Rio blazed out in welcome and familiar city sounds filtered in over the
traffic noise through the car's open windows. Far
beyond Rio were other cities, villages, the great
forest itself. In Rio and beyond were people I
knew, familiar places, the accents and dialects of
a colourful and needy people. And high up on
the mountain, overlooking the teeming city, Rio's
great statue of Christ stood with outspread arms.

I was back.

Montes Claros: The Trail Begins

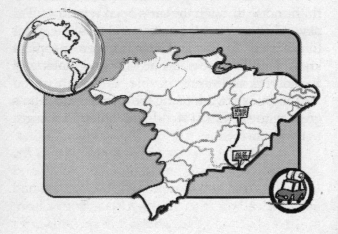

A truck loaded with charcoal swerved across my path, forcing me to yank the steering wheel sharply. My hire car veered to safety with a squeal of brakes. The truck trundled past, its horn blaring. Another vehicle came roaring up behind, a huge lorry carrying crates out of which bedraggled chickens stuck their heads and stared at me. It too passed me in a cloud of dust, petrol and noise.

I'd left Copacabana at 7.30 in the morning, taking the road north from Rio, past the beaches, through the huge tunnel that plunges through the rock on which the statue of Christ stands, on up into the green forested mountains, and down into the flat bush country hinterland.

I was bound for the industrial town of Montes Claros, five hundred miles and at least fifteen hours away, where a journalist called Luiz Ribeiro worked for the *Estado de Minas* newspaper. He had written a number of articles about child prostitution in Montes Claros and the surrounding area.

I'd phoned Luiz from Rio to tell him I was coming to see him. He seemed exactly the right person with whom to begin my investigations.

Mine seemed to be the only small car on the road. The traffic was almost all large trucks and lorries. I wondered sometimes if the drivers had even noticed me. Sometimes a blast from a horn told me that they had, and a few seconds later they would shoot past me with inches to spare, their loads wobbling alarmingly. When I wasn't avoiding collisions with truck drivers, I was negotiating the crumbling verges and large crater-like holes that got bigger the further north I drove. Termite mounds punctuated the fea-tureless landscape.

The sun was high in the sky and my skin was already reddening. The road was a tiny country road linking Rio with the industrial town of Montes Claros, a dusty ribbon reaching out to a hazy horizon, the tarmac already melting in the heat. I resigned myself to a hard day's driving. Loads of charcoal, coconuts and other fruit, and livestock bound for the market or the slaughterhouse, passed me as I drove. It all added to the amount of grit and dust blowing about, especially when the highway shrank to a single lane and one vehicle – usually mine – had to drive along the broken verges to allow another to pass.

Night had fallen by the time I reached the town, which was plunged into gloom by electricity rationing. I had to drive with care.

The small town squares were almost in darkness; a few people out on the streets looked at me without curiosity as I drove cautiously past them looking for a hotel. There wasn't a wide choice. I found one in the town centre, next to a trailer that served as a burger bar. I climbed stickily out of the car, aching and sore from the sweltering heat of the day. I checked in, cleaned myself up and went for a burger. I was starving.

I sat on my own and ravenously gobbled my double-decker cheeseburger with extra everything. Ketchup and mayonnaise splurted on to the table as I ate.

A waiter came and wiped my table. He nodded towards a group of girls sitting at a table in the far corner, and winked at me conspiratorially. I looked back blankly.

The girls were giggling amongst themselves and eyeing me. They were teenagers, around fifteen years old. I suddenly realised what they were doing there, and why there were so many businessmen standing at the bar. I slurped the last of my milkshake noisily and left as quickly as I could.

It was a grim introduction to Montes Claros. I went back to my hotel wondering just how big a task I had taken on.

I woke next morning with my left arm and the whole left side of my face burned red and sore. I winced as I dressed, but resisted the temptation to spend the morning quietly in my room.

At 9 o'clock I walked out of the hotel into blazing sunlight. The streets that had been almost deserted the night before were now thronged with people. Pushing past them as I walked through the town centre, my scorched skin recoiled in protest.

Luiz Ribeiro's office was a simple, functional room at the back of a house he shared with the local TV station. It held a computer, a laptop, a phone and a lot of papers. Luiz was sitting at his desk as I entered: he was a quite short, terse man, with straight hair cropped in a pudding-basin cut, and strikingly heavy eyebrows. He looked up from his laptop as I came in.

'*Senhor* Matt – good morning, good morning, I've been getting things ready for you. Sit down.'

He indicated a pile of folders. 'My articles on child prostitution. You know, it's a very big problem here, very big. Hundreds of girls are selling their bodies. Some of them, just ten years old.'

'How big is Montes Claros?'

'Three hundred thousand – or thereabouts.' He produced the figure instantly. 'Didn't think it was so many? Well, a lot of people come here looking for a better life. Then they find there aren't any jobs here. So they move out to the hillsides – to the *favelas* – and the daughters end up on the streets as the breadwinners.'

The formalities appeared to be over. I opened the folder. Luiz returned to his typing. 'Deadlines,' he explained. He worked at great speed, his whole body lurching as he hammered the keys. He continued to type, on and off, for the duration of our meeting.

The articles were impressive. Luiz had been writing for a long time and had won awards for journalism. He was a 'stringer' – a local correspondent – for one of the biggest newspapers in the state, and two of his articles published there had brought about a parliamentary enquiry into child prostitution in the area. 'They asked me to go and testify,' he told me.

I carried on reading. Much of what he had written was not new to me, but there was plenty that was shocking and suggested further avenues I could explore. I began to form strategies in my mind, making mental notes of people to whom I should be talking and places to which I should go. I was feeling very pleased that I had decided to visit Luiz Ribeiro at the beginning of my investigation.

Then I turned a page and struck gold.

It was a short, single-column piece, told in blunt language without any of Luiz's more extravagant scene-painting. That made it all the more powerful. It contained few details. It was a brief report that the Children's Police squad had raided the home of a local woman. The reason given was that the woman had been accused of auctioning the virginity of a twelve-year-old girl. I gasped involuntarily and sat back in my chair.

Everything seemed to have stopped for a moment. Dust-motes hung frozen in the mid-morning sun streaming through the window; outside in the drab yard, a few sprigs of vegetation were motionless in the airless heat. Luiz fumbled for the return key, completed his sentence, and looked up.

'Found something interesting?'

I indicated the article. 'The auction of the girl.'

Again, he seemed uneasy. 'That was a while ago. They made a big fuss at the time.'

'It's a very short piece,' I said. 'Didn't the paper want any more?'

'It was just a news item.'

'But that's a really big story, just as big as the others about child prostitution. Surely that would have started an enquiry?'

'Oh, you don't want to get involved with that,' he said off-handedly. 'That's *barra pesada* – heavy stuff.'

Then he looked at me, straight in the eyes. 'You could get yourself into serious trouble. Serious trouble.'

I changed tack. 'It must be pretty difficult to write a story like that,' I said. 'What's the real story? Who's really behind it? The woman, Cláudia – did you know her?'

'Everyone knows her,' he grunted. 'She runs an agency. That's what she calls it, anyway. It's a front for procurement. She fixes up wealthy businessmen with young girls.'

Already he was telling me much more than his brief article had contained.

'When she got busted, the police found a list of her clients. There were over three hundred names on it. Well-known businessmen, minor local officials, wealthy landlords, rich factory-owners – it was a long, long list.' The heavy eyebrows were raised expressively. 'The police never questioned any of them. And Cláudia ran away before she could be arrested.'

He shrugged his shoulders and slumped back in his chair. 'That's why you shouldn't ask questions. There are a lot of powerful people involved.'

'How can I find out more? Who should I speak to next?'

'I don't think you should speak to anybody next. You should leave it alone. *Really*.'

I persisted. Finally he sighed heavily, looked at the ceiling, and said, 'Maria Néusa. Talk to Maria Néusa. She was the Children's Police Chief who headed the raid.'

There was nothing more to be got out of Luiz, who was now typing furiously, his arms flailing at the keyboard. The interview was clearly at an end. I said my thanks and left.

I emerged into the bright sunlight. The streets were even busier. I looked at the people differently now: had any of these people been bidders at Cláudia's auction, I wondered?

I trudged across the town centre to the Children's Police Department, where I managed to talk my way into Maria Néusa's office. She was a severe, good-looking woman who stared at me as I introduced myself and interrupted my explanation of why I wanted to talk to her.

'I could not possibly comment.'

All my best efforts to persuade her met with the same stony response. She wasn't defensive; she seemed unruffled by my questions. I was being fobbed off by somebody with superior stonewalling skills. I knew when I was beaten.

I decided to try a different tack, and went to the office of the Juvenile Court judge who had tried the case. He simply passed me on to a junior colleague, who passed me to one of his colleagues, and so it continued. Nobody would talk to me about the virgin auction.

One contact did seem particularly promising, but it came to nothing. I was told of a policeman who had access to the records and who knew about the story. 'Carlos. Talk to Carlos,' I was urged. 'He'll tell you all you need to know.' Full of new excitement I rang Carlos' home every night for a few days. He was never available. Sometimes his wife answered apologetically, sometimes the phone just rang unheeded. I tried his place of work, but again could not locate him. 'Oh – Carlos is away right now, you can't see him...'

Eventually I recognised that all the doors were closed at present, and decided to move on. My next contact had come through Nebson Paixão, a professor at Montes Claros' Unimontes University. He had recently published staggering statistics on prostitution in the Jequitinhonha

Valley east of Montes Claros. His team had counted 4,120 children and adolescents selling their bodies in the Valley, and identified 255 prostitution points along the main highway – mostly petrol station forecourts, tyre shops and roadside brothels. One of those brothels was run by a woman called Cléuza. I decided to visit Cléuza's House.

Chapter 3

Jequitinhonha Valley: The Houses of Hopelessness

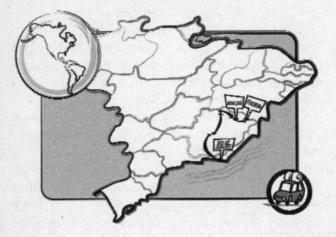

Cléuza's establishment was two drab buildings on a patch of red earth, set back from the BR-251 highway along which I had driven on the long journey east from Montes Claros. Two lorries were parked nearby. Two girls were sitting on the steps of one of the houses, scrubbing clothes.

Another girl squatted on a bench, painting her toenails, her hair wrapped in a towel. I got out of the car.

'What do you want?'

A woman was sitting at a wooden kiosk. I walked up to her and offered her my hand.

'*Dona* Cléuza?'

'Who wants to know?'

'Professor Nebson said you would help me. I'm doing research.'

She smiled and accepted my handshake. 'Well! Why didn't you say?'

Cléuza was a jolly woman, very ready to talk, but there was a sadness about her. Her smiles seemed to conceal some kind of self-condemnation. She was in her mid-fifties, I knew, but looked a lot older.

'This place is like a prison,' she joked. 'None of the girls really want to be here. They're only here because there's nowhere else to go. But they get looked after well. They pay me 45 *reals* a week. They get two meals a day, their bed linen and blankets, and they each have their own room.' She grinned. 'It's a good deal.'

'Where do they come from?'

'Oh, from all over Brazil. They go from one brothel to another, you see. They hitch lifts on the trucks. They get around.' She sighed. 'You know – I feel so sorry for them sometimes. I know what they go through. If they don't end up dead they'll end up like me. I'm not sure which is worse.'

I asked Cléuza how old the girls in her house were.

'You're asking me if I've got underage girls here,' she said sharply. 'Well, the answer's "No". I'm always turning little girls away. They swear to me that they're over eighteen but you can tell they're just kids. Some of them are only twelve – yes, really! Most brothel-keepers wouldn't think twice about taking them. You see, the younger the girls the more customers. But I don't want any trouble.'

Some houses treated their girls like slaves, Cléuza told me. If the girls didn't make their night's quota of clients they were flogged or starved. 'Not me! These girls, I treat like my own daughters. Some days I roast a whole cow for them! You ask any of them. They'll tell you I'm like a mother to them.'

'Come inside,' she said. I followed her into her house. By her bed was a home-made altar, decked with candles and hideous statuettes of evil-looking creatures. Cléuza was a follower of the folk spiritist religion Candomblé.

'Those are my saints,' she said, pointing fondly to the altar figures. 'I pray to them every night. I ask them to forgive me for keeping a brothel.'

'So do you think what you're doing is wrong?'

'Think? I *know* it! What I do is a mortal sin,' she said tightly. 'But I never stop asking for forgiveness. My religion says you can ask 7,777,777 times to be forgiven. Every day I ask my saints to forgive me. But it's never enough. It still weighs heavy on my conscience.'

'How many more times have you got left?' I smiled. Her face crumpled.

'I don't know what I'm going to do when I've used the seven million. Really I don't.'

There was a sombre silence as I tried to think what to say next. I could hear conversation outside.

'May I talk to one of your girls?'

She agreed. The other building was a dormitory block with a row of wooden doors. She pushed one of them open. 'Deane, this is a friend of mine,' she announced. 'You won't mind answering his questions, will you?'

A blonde was sitting, half awake, on an unmade bed. The room was cramped and windowless. It was painted pink, and furnished with the bed and a small chest of drawers piled with shampoo, perfume, lipstick, hairclips and brushes.

'Pleased to meet you,' she said groggily, squinting as the sunlight flooded the room.

Deane was twenty and had worked for Cléuza for six months. She'd been a prostitute for six years. 'I was fourteen. I was playing with some friends by the waterfall and a woman started talking to me. She was from a local brothel; she said she'd pay me two hundred *reals* a day if I went to work for her. I needed the money, so I agreed.'

Deane's price was falling all the time. 'I charge twenty *reals* now. Thirty for a whole night.' Twenty *reals* is about £6. 'My sister's younger than me. She works in a brothel down the motorway. I've got a son, too. He's six months old.'

I looked around the small room. She shook her head.

'He lives with my mother. They're a hundred miles away. I haven't seen him since the day he was born...' Her matter-of-fact, flat narrative trailed off.

'What happens next? What do you want for the future?'

She smiled bleakly and looked around the dreary room. 'It's too late,' she said. 'Maybe one day a trucker will take me away with him. If not, there's no way out of this life for me.'

Most of Cléuza's girls were in the same plight. None of them was over twenty five, and very few held out any hope for the future. The boundaries of their world were the walls of their brothel bedrooms. They regarded themselves as past it, pensioned off, in an industry that idolised childhood.

Roseneide had the singing, north-eastern accent of her home town Petrolina, seven hundred miles to the north. She had started selling herself to foreign tourists in the coastal resort of Recife when she was ten years old. Now twenty-one, she was earning a fraction of what she had made then.

Ângela was nineteen. In her day she had strutted the famous black and white pavements of Copacabana, the darling of the wealthy tourists who prowled about looking for pleasure. 'Sometimes they paid me in American dollars!' she boasted wistfully. 'But I was worth it. I was only thirteen.'

Most of them missed their families, broken up and separated by poverty but still dearly loved. One of the girls, Sirlene, told me how much she missed her daughters. One was three years old, one five, and they lived with their grandmother in a rural village fifty miles away. She took me to one side and offered me a deal. 'Take me to see my children,' she said. 'And on the way, I'll take you to another brothel where I used to work.'

I was well aware that Professor Nebson would not be a name to open every door. I needed to be vouched for by someone who was trusted. I took Sirlene up on her offer.

The journey took three hours, driving through unvarying scenery dotted with villages nestling in the parched hills. Each was approached by a dirt track leading off the main road, a road sign announcing each exotic place name: Dry Waterfall, Lake Long Gone, Fruit of Milk, Brook of Axes, Dull River.

My companion talked unceasingly. Words poured from her, giving me a detailed picture of the lonely life that she and the other girls lived. She was twenty-four, had worked as a prostitute since the age of eighteen, and had graduated from petrol station forecourts to the roadside brothels, where the money was more regular and the work less risky. She had travelled the length and breadth of the Valley many times over.

She was full of lurid anecdotes, all of them ringing horribly true. 'Don't slow down! Keep driving! This part is full of bandits. They hide in the undergrowth, you know, and if you give them a chance they shoot you!'

I was beginning to understand why so many lorries had overturned, taking sharp bends at impossible speeds.

'Cross-eyed Zé used to own this place,' she exclaimed as we passed a boarded-up petrol station. 'The bandits shot him dead last week. Point-blank range. They only got a few *reals* and a tankful of petrol.'

A roadside repair shop triggered another torrent of information. 'You see that boy? His dad died from overdosing on Viagra! He was seventy-six, really he was! Spent every night in the brothels and every night he took Viagra with whisky to keep him going. They say his heart just dried up...'

We left the main motorway and took a smaller road to a village named Inside Cattle Pen. The road led through dense forests of eucalyptus. Thin spires of smoke from charcoal furnaces rose from deep in the trees and sent a pungent aroma across the road. Soon the tarmac gave way to a rough dirt track. We drove on in clouds of orange-red dust.

A few miles before Inside Cattle Pen we stopped in an empty truck park. In its far corner was a brick building with a corrugated iron roof. A painted wooden sign swung creakily in the evening breeze. It read: 'Bar of the Little Girls.'

The interior was badly lit and gloomy. Chairs were upturned on metal tables and broken beer bottles crunched under our feet. A girl was drying beer glasses behind the bar. When she saw us she ran to hug Sirlene.

'This is Daiane. She's Deane's sister.'

'You'll have to be quick,' warned Daiane. 'Baiano's back any minute, and if he finds you here there's no telling what he'll do.'

Baiano was the kind of unscrupulous and violent brothel owner Cléuza had warned me about. If a girl refused to work she would go without food and if that didn't work he would beat her with a broom handle or leave her, terrified, in the forest for the night.

Though a childish, mini-skirted seventeen, Daiane was not the youngest in the house. 'A thirteen-year-old *novata* arrived from Montes Claros yesterday. Baiano doesn't care about the law and the police don't come out here anyway. We're in the middle of nowhere here.'

It was Deane, she said, who started her in prostitution. 'I was twelve. She phoned me and said she had a job for me in Cândido Sales in Bahia State. When I got there, Deane told me the job was in a brothel used by the rich local landowners. I was terrified at first, but Deane said I'd get used to it. She was right.'

Before long, everyone wanted Daiane. 'I had more money than I'd ever had in my life. I could buy the things I'd dreamed of, even send money back to my family.'

But nothing could hold back the clock. As she grew into her teens, Daiane's price plummeted. Soot-stained truckers used her now, their bodies ingrained with charcoal. You could buy Daiane for just fifteen *reals*, and even then she had to compete with younger girls. She could barely pay the rent. Daiane too had a daughter, seven months old and living with her mother in Medina.

A younger girl walked into the saloon, a towel draped round her neck. This was Kelly, the new thirteen-year-old. She was as ready to chat as Daiane had been.

'I was living at home in Montes Claros. I hitched a lift with a man driving a charcoal truck. My family? – they couldn't care less. They're probably glad I've gone.'

'Surely not,' I ventured. 'After all, you're their daughter. They must be sick with worry.'

She shrugged. 'Last time I saw my mother she told me I was no daughter of hers. That's why I left. I just packed my things and walked out.'

'What will you do now?'

She crossed her arms smugly. 'Nothing.' She smiled lazily. 'I'm going to stay here and make a lot of money. That will show my family I can do without them.'

I did not fancy Kelly's chances. If Professor Nebson's research was any guide she would probably never earn enough to keep herself from going hungry. Of those he had interviewed, 73 per cent said they charged less than twenty *reals* a time, a third of them charged just ten *reals* – about three English pounds. The money barely paid for their daily subsistence. According to Nebson's findings, by the time she was sixteen Kelly would have performed at least two abortions on herself, using a knitting needle or coat-hanger. Besides the grave risks of injury from those amateur procedures, she would, over her teenage years, have contracted any number of sexually-transmitted diseases and would have a high risk of AIDS infection. Her chances of surviving to adulthood were slender.

Perhaps the most disturbing of Nebson's findings was this: 36 per cent of the girls questioned said that they would never leave the roadside brothels, even if they were given other opportunities to earn money. They felt that they were not capable of achieving a better life and did not deserve to. Put simply, the brothels were houses of hopelessness.

The time had flown. Baiano must surely be on his way back now, and I had not forgotten Daiane's dark warnings about his attitude to unwanted visitors. Sirlene and I said goodbye to Daiane and Kelly and went back to the car. As I started the engine Baiano arrived with a great screeching of brakes, his rusting *Brasília* roaring to a halt outside the bar. We drove off hurriedly, conscious of Baiano's icy glare pursuing us.

'*Mamãe!*'

'We didn't know you were coming!'

'You're really back! You're not to go away again – never, never, never!'

As soon as they saw her Sirlene's daughters had hurled themselves at her, squealing with delight. Now they were hugging her tightly, as if, diminutive as they were, they might be able to keep her with them and prevent her from leaving again. I watched Sirlene holding them, stroking their hair, whispering endearments to them. My eyes filled with tears. Hours with

Sirlene on the road, listening to her tireless talking, had not convinced me that Sirlene needed to do what she did; nor that she had no reason to leave behind her life in the roadside brothels. The only reason she needed was right in front of her: her beautiful, bright-eyed daughters. But tomorrow she would be back at Cléuza's House.

Sirlene's mother lived with the girls in a village nestling in the hills. It was called Lake Underneath – an optimistic name, for the place was parched and there was not a lake in sight. Today a crowd of women and barefoot toddlers had gathered excitedly in the main square: there was going to be a roast chicken auction.

'Will you be staying for the chicken auction?' asked Sirlene's mother. I politely refused. The light was fading now and I needed to get on.

I drove back down the tortuous route round the hills and rejoined the motorway which veered southwards into the river valley. At Araçuaí, a medium-sized town on the banks of the Jequitinhonha River, I found a place to stay the night. I saw little of Araçuaí, however, as electricity rationing meant the streetlights were turned off and the town was in pitch darkness.

Next morning I embarked on the thirty-mile journey to Medina, the town where, Daiane from the Bar of Little Girls had told me, her mother lived.

At one village on the way I gave a lift to an elderly woman who was trudging along the road, laden with bags. As she clambered into the car she was beside herself with gratitude, calling down innumerable blessings on me. She was a sad example of how hard life was for the elderly in these remote regions. There was, of course, no public transport at all. If you did not own a horse you went everywhere by foot. And she had no resources to see her through difficult times.

'I pray every day for the rains to come,' she said. 'I haven't got a well. If there's another drought I'll be the first to die of thirst.'

She told me she was going to the next village. I left her there, after helping her lift her assortment of bags out of the car.

'The Lord bless you,' she said. 'You've been very kind.'

As I drove on, I wondered whether she was an angel. I cherished her blessings, coming from one who was typical of the disadvantaged people of the Valley. She was a necessary reminder that the statistics I had read were not simply lists of facts and figures but records of real people.

Those statistics are indeed horrifying. Of every thousand children born in the Jequitinhonha Valley, 58 die before their first birthday – a mortality rate 45 per cent higher than the national average. Those who survive their first year weigh 60 per cent less than normal babies. Half the Valley's population is illiterate, a third of all families receive only half the minimum wage, and two-thirds of the population suffers from chronic malnutrition. While rich kids in Rio eat American fast food and play Japanese video games, the children of the Valley die of African diseases like kwashiorkor – an advanced form of starvation that bloats the infant's body and destroys its immune system.

This is the irreconcilable tragedy of Brazil. In a country so rich in resources, new-born babies are dying of hunger and young girls are trading their innocence for a plate of food.

Medina sprawled along the margins of the BR-116 motorway. The tall chimney of a granite quarry overshadowed endless rows of wattle-and-daub cottages. On one side smoke poured from the factory, on the other fumes billowed from the lorries on the motorway. The air was foul, and Medina was smothered in a heat that sapped every ounce of strength.

Daiane had given me her mother's address. I found the house, in the middle of a long terrace of identical mud-brick cottages. A young woman was leaning out of a window. I pulled up outside the house.

'Excuse me – is this where Daiane's mother lives?

The woman looked puzzled.

'Daiane – she works in a bar, near Inside Cattle Pen. She said her mother lives here.'

'Oh! *That* Daiane. She doesn't have a mother. At least, not one to speak of.'

The woman introduced herself as Márcia. She invited me into her house for a coffee. Márcia told me Daiane's real story. It was a sad one. I was to hear many like it in the weeks that followed.

The house Daiane had directed me to was not hers, but the home of a family who were looking after her new-born baby. The truth was that Daiane's mother had herself been a prostitute and had abandoned her daughter at birth. Daiane had been raised by another woman, who in turn had disowned her when she started selling her body on the streets.

Daiane and Deane were not sisters, Márcia explained. Daiane was not seventeen years old, but fifteen – she was using another girl's identity card to conceal her age. Two days ago she had appeared unexpectedly at Márcia's house and taken her baby back with her to the brothel.

As Márcia in her matter-of-fact way recounted Daiane's story, I began to understand why girls like Deane and Daiane were falling so easily into the prostitution trap.

'Most of the teenage girls in Medina are prostitutes,' she told me. 'That's a normal occupation here. As soon as a girl starts puberty – sometimes before then – she's expected to start "working". The mothers stay at home, the fathers earn almost nothing at the granite quarries. So the girl is expected to head for the motorway. The money she makes there can make the difference between her family going hungry, and scraping a living.'

Márcia herself was no exception. 'I started work as a prostitute when I was twelve,' she said. 'My sister's thirteen – she's already making money on the motorway.' A troubled look passed over Márcia's face, the first sign of concern in the whole conversation. 'She's pregnant ... I suppose she'll have to deal with it. It goes with the job. If you're careful you can get rid of it and not get ill.' She shrugged. 'Yes, I reckon she'll be OK. There are plenty who'll be able to tell her what to do.'

I left Medina unable to forget Márcia's parting words: 'There's no hope here in the Valley. The only hope a girl has is to be found on the motorways, at the petrol stations and in the truckers' cabins.'

4

Governador Valadares: The One-Ninety-Nine Girls

'You simply can't do the trip without coming here,' Abigail had insisted when I rang her to tell her about my plans.

Abigail was the leader of the Children's Council in Governador Valadares. I had known her since my work with street girls in Belo

Horizonte. Many of the girls who lived rough on the streets of Belo came from Valadares, making the journey hidden inside freight trains bound for the state capital. Through our work some of the girls returned to their homes. But for every girl we sent home, another one or two arrived back on the streets. There were five children's councillors working full time in Abigail's department and they could not cope with the number of new cases that arrived on their desks every day.

Valadares has a number of attractions that have made it an unlikely tourist centre. For example, the town has some of the most peculiar winds in the world. Hang-gliders and paragliders from all over the world come here, attracted by the huge *cumulo-mugus* – hot air that rises in strange twists and creates unusual turbulence. A number of international competitions are hosted by the town, the most spectacular of which is the hanggliding World Cup.

Valadares is also famous for its semi-precious stones. Hidden beneath the lacklustre landscape, encrusted in underground caves, are some of the world's richest reserves of gems and minerals. Diggers come from all over the world to chisel out their own specimens. And those whose mineral tastes are more scientific than cosmetic come to scour the ground for meteorites from Mars. In 1958 one of the only ten 'red planet' rocks ever discovered was found in Governador Valadares.

I arrived on the outskirts of the town and for a diversion (and a cool respite from the morning sun) drove up the Ibituruna, a plug of volcanic rock that juts out from the flat river valley. A group of reluctant hang-gliders was preparing to leap from a thousand-foot high cliff edge. After more than an hour, none of them had summoned up the courage to make the jump. Rather disappointed, I made the steep descent back into the stuffy mid-morning heat and spent the rest of the morning window-shopping in the few busy town-centre streets.

The Valadares shopper has really only two choices of where to spend his or her money: the gemstone shops and the 1.99 shops. In the former you can buy rough and cut stones of every size and type – green tourmalines, red rubies and bright-blue topaz, and none of them selling for less than 100 *reals*. You can also buy mineral sculptures, delicate figurines of genies, goddesses, aliens, bears and other strange creatures fashioned in minerals like jasper and dolomite.

The 1.99 shops are crammed with plastic toys, furry animals, fake mobile phones, cut-price clothes and hundreds of other cheap Paraguyan imports, all for a single, knock-down price. They are the commonest shops in town and, to judge by the crowds of shoppers rummaging in the bargain bins, the most popular.

They were also more within my price range than the gemstone shops, and I spent most of the rest of the morning there. I bought a furry pen with a flashing top and carried my trophy back to my hotel, the São Salvador.

In the afternoon I went to see Abigail. Her desk was piled high with files and folders. She gave me a bleak run-down of the situation in Valadares. In 2000 the Children's Council had attended 184 cases of child prostitution involving children of between ten and fourteen years of age. By the end of 2001 the number had soared to four hundred and was still rising. And these were only the cases that had come to the Council's attention – the real figure was certainly much higher.

'What does that name mean?'

I pointed to a folder on Abigail's desk that bore the scribbled label '1.99 girls'.

'It's the nickname they give to girls who sell their bodies on the motorways. You've seen those 1.99 shops that sell all those hideous cheap things?'

I hid my flashing pen.

'They call them the 1.99 girls because they're cheap and worthless. That's what they say – and the girls end up believing it.'

I looked through some of the files and read some of the stories they contained.

Janete – fourteen years old, living with her father, mother and three brothers. Her father organised drinking competitions for his sons and gave prizes to the one who downed most beer or *cachaça* rum. When drunk, Janete's brothers often beat her up or tried to rape her. At twelve she had begun to let men grope her for money. Now she sold her body on the motorway, often leaving home for days on end. She had been to the Children's Council three times looking for advice about sexually-transmitted diseases she had contracted.

Sabrina – sixteen. Her mother had been a prostitute and had died when Sabrina was seven. Sabrina and her brother had gone to live with an aunt who was constantly shouting abuse at her. She often said, 'Go to the motorway like your vagabond mother!' As soon as she could, Sabrina left her aunt's house and went to live with a group of female friends. Every night they went to the motorway where they sold sex to truck drivers for just ten *reals* a time. Sabrina was pregnant and had no idea who the father was.

Sâmia – thirteen. She was found by the Children's Council renting a room in a cheap town-centre hostel. She said she had come to Valadares from a nearby town to make money by selling her body. She claimed her parents did not care about her. Angry that the Children's Council had foiled her money-making scheme, she ranted, 'I've got lots of clients in high places – businessmen, even policemen. So don't think you're going to stop me.'

'Do you think I would be able to talk to one of these 1.99 girls?'

Abigail thought for a moment. Then she handed me a file. 'That's Leidiane,' she said. 'She's thirteen.'

Leidiane lived in a huge *favela* shanty town on the outskirts, called Tourmaline. It was a vast eyesore. Named after the translucent gemstone by somebody with a warped sense of humour, Tourmaline was a squalid collection of shanty shacks and red-brick buildings strewn haphazardly over a huge mound of red earth. It looked like a giant mud slide, with people crawling over the hillside like ants and vultures circling overhead.

The dirt track to the foot of the hill ran between the motorway and the open-top refuse tip. The mound itself was criss-crossed with electric cables. Close up, the shacks perched precariously on the muddy slopes. Rubbish was piled in heaps along the track; at places the stench of rotting animal carcasses bit at the back of my throat, making me choke.

I located Leidiane's house halfway up an almost vertical side of the hill. As I approached the red-brick house my legs were aching. I clapped my hands in the customary way and Leidiane's mother appeared from behind a rotting wooden door.

Leidiane was scrubbing clothes on a concrete washboard. She had a baby face, large brown eyes and a bulging belly. At just thirteen, Leidiane was seven months pregnant.

'She's a hard worker,' said her mother, as Leidiane wrestled with slopping garments, banging them against the rough board. 'But she's got a problem. She has a bad nature. I don't know where she gets it from, I really don't. Leidiane, come and talk.'

She put down the washing and told me her story. The oldest of ten brothers and sisters, she often had to look after them on her own; she had no idea who her father was or where he might be, and her mother struggled to find money to feed the large family. She was an entrepreneur in a small way, acquiring used clothes and selling them to other *favela* dwellers. But there was not much money to be made that way. 'So I began to go on to the motorway,' said Leidiane. 'You can make money on the motorway.'

She was eleven when she began selling her body. She joined three other girls from Tourmaline: sixteen-year-old Solange, fourteen-year-old Jordânia and eleven-year-old Paulinha. Every night this gang of four went to Ceasa, the town's food stockpile, where trucks unloaded their cargoes of perishable goods. 'I charged five *reals*, sometimes less. It depended how badly I needed the money.'

She had travelled miles up and down the BR-116 motorway, hitching lifts with drivers. 'They would pick me up, pull up in the middle of nowhere, and afterwards just leave me there in the pitch dark. So I would cross over to the other side of the motorway and wait for another truck to take me back.'

One of those truck drivers was the father of Leidiane's baby, though she could not remember which one it had been, and he was probably hundreds of miles away by now. His ten-minute five-*real* fling with the young 1.99 girl outside Tourmaline was far from his thoughts now. For him it had been a moment's entertainment, like a go on a slot machine or downing a bottle of *cachaça*. For one poor, frightened girl, however, that night's misadventure would probably cause distress and pain for generations to come. Would the baby – a fiver's worth of unprotected sex – grow up to be a 1.99 girl like her mother?

If good intentions could achieve success Leidiane was in with a chance. 'I'm going to be a good mother,' she assured me. 'I'm going to bring up my child well. I'm finished with working the motorway. No more thumbing for lifts on the hard shoulder!' She patted her tummy protectively. 'Not like the others,' she said dismissively. 'They're still down at Ceasa every night.'

But the odds were cruelly stacked against her. A few minutes' conversation made it clear that Leidiane knew nothing about being pregnant and even less about rearing a child.

Her mother told me that she herself had been a 'woman of the night'; Leidiane was the unwanted consequence of a cheap liaison in a trucker's cabin. I watched this protective mother and her industrious house-proud daughter and once again my heart was crushed to see the old pattern operating. So many children I'd met were following in their mother's footsteps. What chance did any of them have, when puberty was just another earning opportunity and childhood something that passed fleetly by, like a beautiful landscape seen briefly from the window of an express train?

I decided to find the other members of Leidiane's gang. Solange was easy to locate. She lived in the next road. But she was not home when I called. She'd left early, leaving her new-born baby with her mother. 'She's gone to the Black Hole. I get so worried when she goes there. Two girls were murdered there last week.'

The Black Hole was a *boca-de-fumo*, a place where drugs were bought and sold. Solange, like her best friend Jordânia, was involved with a dangerous gang of drug dealers.

The house where fourteen-year-old Jordânia lived, just around the corner from Solange, boasted a cast-iron door. I banged hard. She erupted from her bedroom, her hair – dyed a patchy blonde – tangled and matted. I said I'd come from Solange's house.

'Don't mention that *piranha* here,' she snarled. 'The bitch accused me of sleeping with her baby's father. As if I'd stoop that low!' This was just a temporary hiccup in their relationship, Jordânia conceded, but in the meantime if Solange dared to come near the house she'd get her eyes scratched out.

The third member of the gang was also not at home when I called. Eleven-year-old Paulinha lived with her mother in a tiny room at the end of a dark alleyway at the foot of the hill, where rubbish and effluent washed down when the rains came. The place stank. Paulinha's mother greeted me suspiciously. 'She isn't here. She's gone to Inhapim. She won't be back until Thursday.'

'What's she doing in Inhapim?'

The woman looked at me sharply, as if suspecting I was being deliberately stupid. 'Why do you want to know?'

There was only one reason why anyone would go to Inhapim, it turned out. The place was a roadside brothel fifty miles down the motorway. Paulinha worked there regularly for two or three days at a time, while her mother waited back home for her eleven-year-old daughter to return with the next month's grocery money.

I trudged back out of Tourmaline. The stifling cocktail of traffic and industrial fumes seemed almost healthy by comparison with the reek of decay and filth that I was leaving behind.

As the precarious heap of dwellings faded into the distance I was lost in thought. How could a mother make her daughter sell her own body? What did sex mean to these young children, used and brutalised from before the first stirrings of womanhood? What lay ahead for them? Would they ever have relationships in which physical love-making was the joy and deep mystery it was supposed to be – or was sex going to be for the rest of their lives just a handful of loose change? And what of those who kept this evil system in place, from the truckers who treated the young prostitutes purely as objects of passing pleasure, to those who could do something to help the girls but chose not to do so?

Like Gideon facing a mighty army with just a handful of men, I wondered what possible impact any individual could have, against the faceless powerful structures that defeated, with frightening ease, the efforts of government, local jurisdictions and the voluntary sector to bring it all to an end.

⌘ ⌘ ⌘

Cecília woke from a drugged sleep to find padded silk surrounding her. There was no light, no sound beyond her hoarse breathing. Slowly she began to grasp the horror of her situation. Her plan had worked – worked too well; she'd feigned death to avoid marrying the man she despised and now her true love Valentim was weeping inconsolably by her tomb. Which was where Cecília was right now. As realisation dawned she cried out, her voice weak from the drugs, pushing desperately against the pillows and finding only unyielding wood beneath. Above, Valentim heard her faint cries and began digging frantically in the sticky earth until his fingertips were raw and bleeding.

Then the phone rang.

Brazilian TV soap opera is a genre all its own. Most of the plots seem to be taken straight from Shakespeare plays, and the melodrama is piled high. These *novelas* thrive on the cliff-hanger, the teaser that keeps you coming back for more. Lying on my hotel bed I'd been engrossed in the latest episode of *A Padroeira*, the six o'clock soap, and though I was fairly sure that Cecília was going to survive, the phone was an unwelcome interruption.

'Do you want to help us catch a pimp?'

Abigail's voice was as calm as if she was offering me a drive in the mountains.

A Padroeira seemed, all of a sudden, to be no longer so interesting. 'She's called Fátima,' explained Abigail. 'She arranges young girls for tourists. She lives in a squat in a *boca-de-fumo*, in a warehouse near the river. Meet us at the corner of Parasol Street and Ângelos.'

The whole team of councillors arrived in a minivan driven by Pablo, the Council's driver. 'Here's the plan,' said Abigail. 'You're a foreign hang-glider. Pablo's a hang-glider too. You're here for the gliding event. You want Fátima to fix you up with some young girls.'

Pablo and I approached the warehouse on foot, along dark and empty streets. A steel panel in the warehouse wall had been forced open. We climbed through the makeshift doorway.

Inside it looked like a scene from hell. A cardboard city had been built from boxes and pieces of wood nailed together, dividing the squatters and their few belongings into their own spaces. There was no light apart from candles dimly flickering and blue circlets of gas flames where people were cooking rice and beans. There was no way of knowing how many families were crammed into the dark shadows. Barefoot children were running everywhere, their screams echoing in the vast hollow interior. I asked some of them if they knew Fátima. They ran off to fetch her. A few nearby faces watched us out of the gloom without much interest.

Fátima was gaunt and scruffy, her clothes dirty and ragged. We shook hands and I explained what we wanted. In the noise nobody could have overheard our conversation, but a hidden microphone in my pocket recorded what was said.

'I can get you two sisters. I'll need some time, though.'

'How old?'

'Thirteen and fourteen. They're very pretty.'

'All right. How much?'

'We can talk money when they arrive. Half goes to me, half to the girls.'

'OK. What time do we collect them?'

'Come back in an hour and a half. I'll go and get them right now.'

It seemed we had a deal. It was eight o'clock. We had until 9.30 to get the police into position and decide what to do next. I asked Fátima one more question. 'Might there be a problem with the police? We don't want any trouble ...'

'Oh no,' she assured us. 'No problem at all. The police never bother us here.'

Fátima clearly did not suspect a thing. When Pablo and I returned to collect the girls, Abigail and the rest of the Council team were waiting in a police van parked just around the corner. Abigail rehearsed me for my big moment. As soon as Fátima handed the girls over I was to give the signal. The police would then move in and catch her red-handed.

My heart was racing as we climbed once more through the narrow gap in the warehouse wall. I knew that if anybody suspected that we were informants we would be in very serious danger. Inside the place was darker and much quieter. The air was filled not with the stewing of beans but with the strong smell of cannabis. Fátima appeared from behind a curtain. Behind I could see a group of men, sitting in a smoky mist, taking drags on a joint. She seemed different now, less businesslike and more relaxed. Much more relaxed, I realised; she was slurring her words.

'C'mon, let's share a joint before you go,' she said languidly. She nodded towards the smoke-filled room. The men looked at us. There was no way I was going further into that darkness.

'Uh – no, we're in a hurry, I'm afraid. Got to get back. Haven't we, Pablo?'

Pablo nodded furiously. I was already feeling trapped. My heart was beating even faster. As Fátima considered my hasty apology I wondered for a moment if our cover had been blown. Then, to our enormous relief, she shrugged her shoulders and went to get the girls.

They followed her out of the gloom. Both were short and plump, both had matted Afro hair, both wore lycro shorts and top. They were sisters: Valcelene and Valdirene.

We emerged into the street, followed by the girls. I took Fátima to a nearby streetlight to talk about payment.

'Fifty *reals* for each girl,' she said, her eyes daring me to challenge the exorbitant price. She was relying on my ignorance; as a foreign tourist I might not know that you could get a young girl for a tenth of that without looking very hard. If I wanted to argue I would get the rough edge of her tongue, of that I was sure.

But I didn't want to argue; the money would never be paid anyway. Fátima handed over the girls and I produced my wallet.

It was the sign the police had been waiting for. The van hurtled round the corner, lights flashing and siren blaring. Everybody froze as it screeched to a halt. Four policemen leaped out, shouting and waving their revolvers. We were all arrested and thrown inside the police van.

It had been decided that for Pablo's sake our real identities would not be revealed to Fátima and the girls – Pablo, as the Council's minibus driver, was a regular visitor to Fátima's part of town. It would be very dangerous for him if he were ever recognised. So we both remained handcuffed in the van for nearly three hours, while Fátima was taken into the police station and formally charged.

We over-acted terribly. Pablo was the worst, wailing and sobbing heartrendingly. I added my own grief. 'What am I going to *do*? I'll miss the competition tomorrow.' I plunged my head into my hands and groaned dramatically. I had picked up a few acting ideas of my own from Cecília and Valentim. 'We're being arrested – and you're thinking about flying?' exclaimed Pablo.

Next to us, Abigail was trying to pretend she did not know us. But she was barely stifling her giggles. The police too joined in the amateur dramatics: one pretended to hit Pablo in the face, using the old theatrical trick of slapping his own hand with his fist. Pablo screamed like an Oscar winner and the girls winced in horror.

Fátima was certainly not pretending. She was dragged, weeping and wailing, to a cell in the police station basement, where she would stay until her court hearing. The evidence – part of which was the tape recording I had made – was overwhelming. According to the Penal Code, Fátima was due for three to eight years in prison for the crime of procuring minors for prostitution.

The two girls were returned to their home. It was explained to them that they must attend the Council's *Sentinela* programme that provides counselling and occupational therapies to child victims of sexual exploitation and abuse.

Sentinela is a state-sponsored scheme based in the towns and cities with the highest incidence of child prostitution. It works from centres that are very well equipped and staffed by expert counsellors. The programme is an example of the huge efforts that the Brazilian government is making to deal with prostitution. The case of Fátima, on the other hand, is an example of how the efforts of the state are constantly being thwarted by corrupt local officialdom, by police who turn a blind eye, and by other people along the line who benefit from the continued existence of this tragic trade.

A few days later I saw Valcelene, the younger of the two sisters, again. She wandered into a bakery close to my hotel while I was sipping a shot of strong coffee. She tried to slip away without my seeing her. I called her over. 'It was a set-up,' I explained. 'Pablo and I were plants. It was all rigged, just to catch Fátima.'

'I knew it! You were all laughing too much.'

'My bad acting, I'm afraid ... Would you like a Coke?'

She told me her story. The girls' father had abandoned them while they were babies. Their mother had been shot dead earlier in the year. Their older brother had run up debts with the drug dealers: they'd come looking for him with guns. His mother had shielded his body with her own, taking the bullet that had been meant for him. 'She was just like that,' said Valcelene. 'She'd do anything for us.'

After their mother's death the sisters lived with their brother, who was still an addict. He paid for his habit by street fighting and burglary. 'There's never enough money for food. If we didn't have what I and my sister earn on the streets, we'd starve.'

She was pleased, she said, that Fátima was now behind bars. Fátima, who was a pimp for hundreds of girls, kept most of the money for herself. If I actually had paid 50 *reals* for Valcelene, she would only have received a few *reals* of it.

It was a story that was becoming too familiar: Valcelene and her sister had turned to prostitution because they had very few options, and Fátima had exploited that lack. But there was a glimmer of hope. The sisters were now being mentored by professionals at the *Sentinela* programme. If Valcelene and Vadirene really wanted help, they were now no longer on their own.

I had reached the end of my week in Governador Valadares. It was time to return my hired car and take the gruelling three-day bus journey to Recife, on Brazil's north-eastern coast, over a thousand miles away.

Before I left, I went back to Ibituruna for the opening of the hang-gliding championships. The sky was cloudless, and crystal blue like a topaz stone. I watched a glider make a running jump over the edge: he floated gracefully into the distance, then climbed in spirals, up towards the dazzling sun.

I thought how many tourists come to Governador Valadares to fly overhead or to burrow underground; yet few know what is really going on at ground level. Thousands of young girls have been tossed into the bargain bin of prostitution, and branded with a name that means worthless and disposable. Most of the 1.99 girls ended up believing it.

Yet it was the price tag that was really worthless. To God these lives were worth far more than the richest exhibits in the gemstone shops. Not one of those children, huddled in darkness waiting for the brief trauma that would put a few coins into the family purse, was unseen by him. The biblical image of the sparrow, whose fall is seen and grieved over by the Creator, has never seemed so apt as it did when I visited the homes and workplaces of the children who were being exploited. Truckers brutally using pre-pubescent girls – mothers forcing their children into prostitution – children whose childhood was being destroyed by nightmare experiences of murders, drugs and violence – and perhaps worst of all, the brief account in Luiz Ribeiro's files of the virgin auction in Montes Claros.

I had tried telephoning my tip-off, Carlos, every night from my hotel but had had no luck. I decided that I would not leave Valadares without making one more effort to contact the elusive Carlos. But I met with exactly the same brick wall. Nobody wanted to put me in touch with Carlos, and I was as far as ever from finding out more about Cláudia and her highly-placed three hundred-strong clientele.

My characteristic impetuosity suddenly kicked in. I made a snap decision. I would postpone my trip to Recife for a few days. I would go back to Montes Claros to look for Carlos. The virgin auction was too big a story to abandon. It was a prime example of people in authority, implicated in shocking abuse of children, and protected by corrupt local officialdom. Find the end of that particular string, I reasoned, and it might lead me further in to the heart of the darkness whose fringes, I knew, I had barely touched.

5

Montes Claros Again: The Virgin Auction

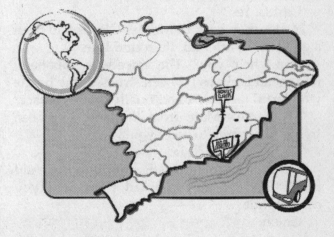

Montes Claros was as busy as ever. It seemed a somewhat cleaner and sweeter place than some of those I had travelled to in the past three weeks, even though by now I had some idea of what went on there. I had come via Rio, where I had left the hire car and taken a bus – an eventful episode. It rained torrentially the whole time and there were massive floods in Rio and the region. Stories of houses disappearing in mudslides were being featured in the world's media.

I arrived safely back in Montes Claros and rang Carlos again from my hotel. My finger was by now so used to dialling his number fruitlessly that it could probably have done so in my sleep. To my astonishment, this time a man's voice answered.

'Carlos. Yes?'

My journey back to Montes Claros had been a good move after all. I'd found him.

'Can I help you?' The voice was impatient; understandably, as I'd been struck dumb by the wonderful fact that I had finally made contact.

'My name's Matt, from England. I've been trying to arrange to meet you.'

'Right – my wife said.'

'I'm doing some investigation into the child prostitution industry in Brazil. I wonder if you can help me?'

'Go on.'

'I was told you had been involved in the action against the virgin auction that was broken up by the police recently.'

'Yes, I can give you a few details.'

'Great! When can I come and see you?'

'Where are you now?'

I told him.

'Well, you can meet me here at the police station. I'll expect you in five minutes.'

I probably made the short journey through the town-centre streets in four.

Carlos was in his late thirties, with neat permed frizzy hair and a small goatee beard. He wore a white short-sleeved shirt buttoned tightly across a spreading beer-belly. He was quite unlike how I had imagined him, not least because I had expected to have to persuade him to help me. But Carlos was very accommodating. When I arrived he was waiting for me. He took me straight into the yard where a battered Ford Cortina was standing. He gestured to me to get in, climbed in himself and started the engine.

'The girl who was auctioned is called Sabrina,' he said. 'I'll take you to where she lives. Only, you must not say that it was me who helped you.'

The journey was eventful. The old Cortina struggled as we drove through a run-down district not far from the centre and approached a steep hill. The engine, which had complained bitterly throughout our short journey, finally spluttered to a halt as the hill came into view. The car shuddered, coughing mutinously as Carlos gave me directions.

'I will have to leave you here' – he glared at the Cortina – 'but you can find Sabrina's house easily. She lives about halfway up the hill, on the right. It has a steel door. You can't miss it.'

I thanked Carlos, still marvelling over the way things had so quickly fallen into place, and started up the steep road. There were a dozen or so houses on the right-hand side, all crudely built – and all with steel doors. I knocked on several before I discovered where Sabrina's family lived. An elderly woman, Sabrina's mother, opened the door.

'Sabrina's playing with her friends in the road. Hold on – I'll call her.'

'No, *Senhora*. It's no problem. I'll go and speak to her there.'

I climbed to the top of the hill and found a group of teenagers playing football, boys against girls. I asked for Sabrina. A girl aged about twelve years old came running over, still out of breath from her exertions with the ball. She was wearing a red and black football shirt with the logo of Flamengo, one of Rio's top teams, like any kid playing in an English town street wearing a Manchester United shirt.

She was a striking girl, very articulate and unusually light-skinned. Unusual, because in Brazil, the poorest people are usually the ones with the darkest skins. Add to this the fact that she was a strong, healthy-looking girl already showing signs of womanhood, and you could see why it was Sabrina who had been chosen to be the centre of the grotesque auction.

'I heard about the auction, Sabrina. I wanted to hear your side of the story.'

'How did you find me? Who told you where I lived?'

'I promised I wouldn't tell. But he said you wouldn't mind. Can I ask you some questions about the auction?'

She sat down beside me on the kerb. 'OK. But you'll have to be quick. We're losing, and I'm our best player.'

As the game proceeded noisily in front of us I asked her how she had first become involved with Cláudia.

'I started doing housework for her – mopping the floor, doing the dishes, things like that. I was happy just to be making some money to help my Mum.'

I was scribbling fast as she spoke. 'What did you think of Cláudia?'

'I didn't know what she did for a living. She was always on the phone, day and night. I thought she must be a lawyer or something like that; she was always going out with men in suits and posh cars.'

'So, when did you find out what she really did?'

'The day she asked me if I was a virgin. That was when she told me about the businessmen. She said she'd pay me 600 *reals*. That's more money than I'd earned in my whole life! She was only paying me 60 *reals* a month for the housework.'

A cheer from the boys announced that the girls had just conceded a goal. They looked despondently at Sabrina.

'I'm going to have to go back.'

'Is there anybody who can tell me more about Cláudia's house and the people who go there?'

Sabrina paused reluctantly and considered. 'There's Viviane. She worked for Cláudia. Works for herself now. Just don't tell her I gave you her number.' She sprinted down the hill again and returned with a mobile phone number written on a scrap of paper. Then she raced back into the football game, immediately took the ball and dribbled it through the legs of the bewildered boys. She shot and scored. The delighted squeals of her team-mates followed me as I walked back down the hill.

'Hello. Is that Viviane?'

'Yes. Who wants to know?'

'My name's Matt. I'd like to talk to you. It's about Cláudia. I'm writing a book.'

There was a silence at the other end before Viviane replied. 'Well, it can't be today. I'm with my solicitor.'

'You've got a solicitor?'

'Not just one. I've got several. I can give you some time tomorrow morning.'

The next day I took a *moto-taxi* to the address she'd given me and quickly regretted doing so.

Perched dangerously on the back of the motorbike, gripping two metal handles, I was almost thrown off several times as it swerved round pot holes and tilted sharply round bends. The bike finally roared to a halt outside Viviane's house.

'I didn't think you'd come.'

The sixteen-year-old was dressed to impress. She wore a black jacket with shoulder pads, a long slit skirt and high heels. Her hair was bleached blonde and her face caked in pale foundation.

We sat down on a plastic-covered sofa. I asked Viviane about Cláudia's clients.

'They were bank managers, car dealers, estate agents – even judges and politicians,' she said. 'Cláudia had lots of friends in high places.'

The girls came from the poor families that struggled to make ends meet, some as young as eleven. 'She used to wait at the school gates, and talk to the girls as they left. She told them they could make lots of money and buy designer clothes.'

'I was talking to Sabrina,' I said. 'She told me she started out like that, doing housework for Cláudia.'

'Sabrina who was auctioned? Yes, I know her.'

'She said she didn't know what Cláudia did. She said it was only when the auction was arranged that she realised what was going on.'

Viviane looked at me oddly. 'She told you that? I suppose she would. It wasn't like that really. Sabrina was a virgin, that's true. But for a while before that, Cláudia paid her to go with men to a motel or somewhere, and play with them. They were allowed to do everything to her. I bet she didn't tell you that.'

The information shocked me, partly because Sabrina had seemed a sunny, articulate child who didn't belong to this world of fumbling and groping in seedy motels; and partly because I had believed her story, and was now discovering that according to her friend it had happened quite differently.

I had to remind myself that it was up to Sabrina how much or little she told a stranger about her sad life. Whether a seasoned temptress or an abused virgin, she was still a victim. It was adults who had set her on whatever she had been doing, and those adults had done so for cash. I began to resent the well-groomed Viviane's cynicism.

But the story that Viviane told was gripping, a sickening account of a nightmare gathering of rich, powerful people and young vulnerable children. Her measured, neutral voice painted a picture of extraordinary depravity.

The idea of the auction had occurred to Cláudia when the Marcos Frota circus came to town. The manager approached Cláudia saying that he wanted to buy a virgin. Cláudia told him about Sabrina. When a price of 800 *reals* was accepted, Cláudia realised that there was a lot of money to be made out of Sabrina's virginity and began phoning round her wealthy clients to see how far she could force the price up.

The sale became an auction. Five of Cláudia's regulars joined in, including Orlando Cunha who owned a large engineering company in the town, and a rich landowner called Klinger. The bidding had been joined by the mayors of three neighbouring towns: Santo Antônio de Retiro, Rio Pardo de Minas and Taiobeiras. I imagined the phone calls, the voices rising in excitement as the price for Sabrina rose, and Cláudia herself, 'rubbing her hands together in delight,' Viviane said drily, as the price soared to 1,300 *reals* – around £400.

'She said she was going to give Sabrina 600 *reals* and keep the rest. Then the police raided her house the day the deal was to be closed. But when they got to her house Cláudia was already well away.'

'How did she know?'

Viviane smiled her cynical smile again. 'I told you, she knows people. She's probably in Bolivia, safe over the border by now.'

I asked her if she knew any other 'agents' I could talk to.

'Sure. Rose, Gisele, Niltinho, Fernandinho, Ricardinho . . . Terezinha's the one you want.

She's taken over most of Cláudia's old clients. She owns a bar in Maracanã. I'll give you her address, provided you promise not to mention me.'

I gave my word.

'And don't, whatever you do, tell her who you really are or what you're doing. If she suspects you at all she'll have you killed. Seriously. Tell her you were one of Cláudia's clients. Tell her you want a girl.'

In Stussi Street in the pleasant middle-class district of Maracanã, nothing seemed out of the ordinary. Children were playing on bikes or rattling skateboards; a small group was sitting on the pavement engrossed in a game of *Tazo*, noisily slamming plastic tokens down. Neighbours stood outside their houses chatting to each other.

Terezinha's bar also seemed quite normal. A man served behind a concrete counter, with a till and a shelf full of spirit bottles. Poster of girls in bikinis advertised Brahma beer; one offered trips to the World Cup in exchange for Coca-cola ring pulls. On the wall, a loud-speaker blasted out the thudding lyrics of *Banda do Tigrão*, a popular funk band with obscene lyrics.

I asked for a Coca-cola.

'We don't sell Coca-cola.'

There was a hint of wariness in his voice. I noticed for the first time that the bottles on the shelf were empty. Terezinha's bar was just a façade, a front to avert suspicion.

I leaned over the counter and whispered confidentially, 'Actually, I'm a friend of Terezinha.' It was the password that Viviane had made me memorise. The man's attitude changed subtly.

'Ah. Right. Please,' he said, lifting the flap of the counter, 'come through.'

We went down a dim corridor stacked to the walls with empty beer crates, and emerged in a spacious room with neatly-arranged red tables and chairs. It looked like a stage set: each table sported an embroidered white cloth, and a loudspeaker was playing gentle music of a kind quite different to that in the fake bar.

'I'll call Terezinha. Would *Senhor* like something to drink?'

'A Coca-cola?'

'Certainly, *Senhor*. One moment, please.'

A few minutes later Terezinha made her appearance. She was an elegant, courteous woman, with meticulously manicured fingernails, freshly permed jet-black hair and lavish red lipstick and nail polish. She was carrying a cordless phone. She greeted me cordially and kissed me on both cheeks. We sat down.

'I used to be one of Cláudia's clients.'

'Oh yes – terrible, terrible thing what happened. At least she managed to get away, eh?'

I nodded. As we made small talk, the phone rang a few times, and Terezinha excused herself and scuttled into a back room where she could be heard negotiating a girl's price or describing, in clinical detail, a child's body. I was beginning to realise that I was getting into deep waters.

'I'm sorry for the interruptions, but you know how it is. My customers are all successful people. Many businessmen, lawyers and civil servants especially.' She looked at me with interest. 'And what do you do?'

'Uh – I'm in the travel business,' I said.

'Oh, tourism. Well, why don't I introduce you to the girls?'

Two young girls appeared from a closed door as if by some prearranged signal and joined me and Terezinha at the table. They both had mobile phones in their hands. Terezinha introduced us. They were sisters, sixteen-year-old Cleidiane, with shoulder length dyed blonde hair, and fourteen-year-old Cristiane, who had short cropped hair and wore a black sequinned top.

In the corridor I caught a glimpse of a small figure with curly blonde hair and a frilly white dress. She seemed even younger than Cleidiane and Cristiane. 'Are there more girls?' I asked.

'Don't you like these pretty ones? Well, I've got more than a hundred. But most stay at home waiting for me to call them.'

Her phone rang again and she left apologetically. I took advantage of her absence to ask the girls some questions.

'How did you get started?'

'We live next door,' said Cleidiane. 'Terezinha offered us a part-time job doing chores in her house. We did that for a few weeks then she asked if we wanted to make more money. She said she'd pay us to go out with some of her rich friends.'

It was an almost identical story to the one Sabrina had told me; obviously this was a common way of recruiting girls. I asked Cleidiane how much she charged.

'120 *reals*. Sixty for me, sixty for Terezinha.'

'I charge 200 *reals*,' bragged Cristiane. 'A hundred for me, and – '

'A hundred for Terezinha? Why is your price higher?'

'Because I'm younger,' she smirked.

'Are you the youngest?'

'Oh no. Some are younger than me. She nodded towards the blonde standing near the stacked crates. 'Alice is a *novata* – she arrived yesterday. She's serving drinks at the moment but when she starts she'll be worth a fortune.'

There was a surreal quality to the conversation, a degree of weird depravity deeper than anything I had yet encountered. Here I was, sitting with two teenage sisters, who had no reason to disbelieve that in a short time I would be having sex with one of them, and they were casually discussing with me how much it

would cost. The pretty tablecloths, the polite
barman, Terezinha's beautifully painted fingernails – everything had the veneer of a pleasant
tea room, a genteel place of conversation and
relaxation. But under the superficial gloss, a
ruthless exploitation and a greediness that
could not care less about the lives that were
being destroyed was at work. I could stand it
no longer and stood up to go.

At that moment Terezinha came back, and
for a moment I felt frighteningly trapped.
'Leaving so soon?' she smiled, and I wondered
whether she had become suspicious. 'Shall we
talk business?'

I calculated the distance across the room to
the corridor, the length of the crated space
through to the bar, and out into the sunlit street.
If I had to make a run for it, it would be a tight
thing if the barman got involved.

But Terezinha, miraculously, seemed to
accept my sudden departure. I said that something had come up, some development that had
to be dealt with right now. Later we could do
business ... 'Sure. It was nice to meet you. Here.
For next time.' She handed me a business card
with her home and mobile numbers.

As I climbed the stairs to my hotel room, I
was still trying to come to terms with what I had
seen. It was one thing to talk to young children
in their comfortable homes and sun-drenched

streets, even when the conversation was about unimaginable abuse, exploitation and suffering. It was different even from the police raid I'd helped to plan on Fátima's dark and impenetrable cardboard brothel. What was so horrifying about my visit to Terezinha's bar was the sheer ordinariness of it: the children outside, playing in the street, and inside, being sold to adults ... nothing else could have illustrated so clearly the extent to which child prostitution was endemic to Brazilian society, ingrained into its everyday fabric, a part of the landscape like the dying beggars in Calcutta whom nobody notices any more because they are so much part of normal life.

I was under no illusions, either, that I had been in serious danger of losing my life in that red-tabled room with its embroidery and gentle music. Had things turned out differently I would have become one of Brazil's statistics, one more tourist who got involved in local crime and was found dead on the streets.

This really was Luiz Ribeiro's *barra pesada*, heavy stuff indeed. I wondered if I had looked too far into the darkness, delved too deep. Suddenly, Montes Claros was no longer a safe place. It was time to get out. I decided to leave as early as I could the next morning, and make my postponed long bus journey to Recife.

I had one more thing to do before leaving. I made a formal report of the names of the three mayors involved in the auction to the state prosecutor in Belo Horizonte responsible for dealing with crimes committed by town and city mayors. The material was later used as the basis of a state investigation into those mayors' involvement with child prostitution. It could not bring back Sabrina's stolen innocence, but I hoped fervently that it would make some impact on the loathsome trade of which she was a victim.

6

Recife: Summertime Cinderellas

At Boa Viagem, Recife's wealthy seaside resort, the beach was littered with melted candles and soggy washed-up roses. The revellers had gone, the fireworks were just ash in the wind. It was New Year's Day 2002, and the beach was already back to normal, full of foreign tourists.

Black beach-peddlers swerved adroitly between them selling cashew nuts, banana chips, prawns and other local delicacies from baskets balanced on their heads.

I was feeling out of sorts, and not just because the celebrations of the night before had made sleep impossible, but also because only two hours before midnight I had arrived in Recife bus station, stiff and sore and headachy at the end of a 35-hour journey.

I had endured the journey sitting next to the on-board toilet compartment, the only seat I was able to get when I booked my ticket at the last minute. The roads to Recife were winding rural ones, and I was flung from side to side as we negotiated the frequent bends. To make matters worse the toilet had started to leak, less than a day into the journey. As I clambered stiffly down the coach steps, all I wanted was a bed and several hours' sleep.

But the streets were full of partygoers, celebrating noisily with firecrackers and bangers. Recognising that it was not going to get any quieter for several hours, I decided to take a taxi to Boa Viagem and find a hotel room.

I had stayed on the seafront watching the celebrations until midnight. On New Year's Eve there are over two million people celebrating on the beaches of Brazil, and Boa Viagem is one of the most popular. People were gathered on the beach, many with tables and marquees for their own private party. Some women were standing at the shoreline, throwing white roses into the waves – a way of appeasing Iemanjá, the god of the sea in the *Umbanda* religion. Other New-Year homages to the mermaid-like goddess include jumping seven waves, lighting candles in the sand and wearing new socks and lucky underwear – red for romance, yellow for prosperity.

I had watched the fireworks lighting up the starry sky and falling back into the sea amidst whoops and cheers. But I was feeling rather short of festive spirit. Besides, I reflected, as I made my way to my hotel, my yellow shirt and bright red shorts might be giving off the wrong signals – and after thirty-five hours on a bus, my underwear was certainly not lucky ...

I strolled along the beachside promenade for a while, stopping at a *barraca* – one of the beach-huts lining the seafront – for a cool coconut-water. The *barraqueiro* held the green coconut expertly in one hand while slicing it open with a carving knife. He managed to do it without spilling a drop – or chopping his hand off.

Recife is a city of 3.3 million people. Few Brazilian cities illustrate so well the saying that Brazil is a paradise for some, purgatory for most, and hell for a few. In a city like Recife, the statistics take flesh very easily. You cannot go far in Recife without remembering that there are ten million children in Brazil who make a living from the streets, including around half a million child prostitutes. In 1999 it was estimated that 540,000 were infected with AIDS.

It is also impossible in Boa Viagem not to notice another aspect of Brazil's sex industry, one that I had not so far seen much of. Recife is a major sex-tourism destination. Foreigners, usually from Europe and mostly Germans and Italians, fly to Recife to have sex with the thousands of prostitutes who work in the city. The sex tourists pay much more than the local people do: one Internet guide to sex holidays in Brazil – 'If any place on this planet comes close to combining sex with excellent cuisine and spectacular beaches and scenery, this is the place to be' – warns readers that the price of sex ranges from $50 with a girl on the street up to '$250 or more with a luscious woman out of the high class strip joints'. This is a different world to that of the children I had met on the motorways, selling their bodies for a handful of *reals*.

For most of the day I wandered up and down the Boa Viagem beachfront, watching the holidaymakers and getting over the long bus journey. In the evening I walked to the Boa Viagem square, where a whitewashed baroque-style church stood uneasily flanked by high-rise hotels. Behind it was a bustling craft fair, where handmade ornaments and brightly-painted souvenirs were being sold.

Along one side of the square was a row of untidy bars, with tables and chairs scattered on the pavement and white-skinned men drinking beer. They watched eagerly as dark-skinned girls, wearing skimpy shorts or miniskirts and Madonna-style bustiers, mingled with them. One of them, a girl in her early teens, wore a frilly white top and tattered blue skirt. She was barefoot. I called her over, and asked her how old she was.

'Thirteen – or fourteen, I'm not sure,' she said, in a contrived baby voice. 'I've never had a birthday. My mum says she's only going to give me a birthday when I'm fifteen.' Her name was Romilda. As we spoke she sucked on a baby's dummy as she spoke and sniffed glue from a plastic bottle.

'I sell my body to help my mum. I give her everything I earn – I don't keep a *centavo* for myself.'

Romilda was very willing to tell me her story. 'I used to polish people's shoes on the square. I hardly earned anything for it. Then my mum got really ill. She needed medicine and that cost money. I was so worried about her. However many shoes I polished, I couldn't make enough to buy what she needed. Then I met a German tourist and he wanted to sleep with me...'

'How old were you then?'

'Eight.'

Prostitution was now a nightly routine for little Romilda. She would sleep until the afternoon then get up and make for the square again. 'I've gone with Germans, Italians, Belgians, Danes, Dutchmen and Englishmen. But I won't do it unless it's with a condom. I don't want to get pregnant, or catch AIDS.'

Romilda had all the wiles of a woman of the streets. She knew a few phrases of English and German – 'You are very beautiful,' she slurred in English. She was fascinated by my dictation machine, and sang into the microphone in Italian – *'Amore mio, amore mio, dolori mio cuore'*. When I played it back to her she squealed with excitement and demanded that I show her how to work the machine. She mastered the controls and recorded several songs, playing them back with great pride. Then she disappeared into the bars, taking my precious digital recorder with her, and I wondered if I had been too trusting.

But Romilda came back, with a tape full of recordings. She played them back to me. One was a heavily German-accented voice: 'Romilda, *puta safada*.' It meant 'dirty bitch' – probably the only two words of Portuguese he had learned.

She had the worldly wisdom of a working prostitute and the captivating innocence of a little girl. She was playful, flirtatious and craved to be the centre of attention. She showed me her favourite dances – samba and *brega* – and her eyes sparkled: 'When I hear music I can't help dancing! And sometimes, when there's no music – I make it up in my head.'

We sat and watched the world go by, Romilda pointing out the men she had slept with that week.

'See him?'

She pointed to a balding, beer-bellied German drinking on a club balcony.

'He promised me one hundred *reals* but I only got ten. He said he'd pay the rest later.' She looked at me slyly. 'Want to go and remind him?'

In front of one of the bars, a fat American was slumped in a chair, puffing on a cigar, watching wide-eyed as a young girl danced for him provocatively. Down the road another tall, red-headed tourist was walking hand-in-hand with one of Romilda's friends, a black girl half his height. They drove off in a taxi.

'See that man over there?'

A burly, heavily-moustached man was walking out of the drugstore. 'That's Jürgen. He's one of my boyfriends.'

'*One* of your boyfriends?'

'Yeah! I've got five.' She counted them on her fingers. 'Four Germans and one Italian.'

'Aren't you supposed to have just one?'

'I can't help it! When I sleep with them I fall in love with them – it's just the way I am!'

Romilda was just a child, playing an adult role. Behind the pretence there was a confused child crying out desperately for help. Over the next few days I got to know Romilda a little. Her mother, I discovered, had beaten her constantly. She had never known her father. One day she took my notebook and drew a childish picture in it. There was a school, a smiling sun, and three stick-figures: a mother, a father and a baby.

I asked Romilda if she had any dreams.

'I've got three,' she answered without hesitating. 'I want my mother to be happy. I want my friends to be happy. And I want a new pair of shoes.'

Later that evening, the girl who had gone off with the red-headed foreigner returned to the square, flourishing a 100-*real* note. Romilda introduced her to me. Her name was Aparecida.

'He took me to a motel,' she told me. 'I think he was French. But he didn't say much, really.'

Aparecida was sixteen years old, and carried an identity card to confirm it. I mentioned that prostitution is illegal in Brazil under the age of eighteen. 'I'm not a prostitute,' she replied. 'They're my *namorados* – my boyfriends. I'm going out with them.'

She said she had been 'courting' men on the square since she was fourteen, and was adamant that she enjoyed her work. She had lived for six months with an Italian, hoping that he would marry her and take her abroad. But he left and went back to Italy without her.

'One day I'll find my Prince Charming.'

'I've already found mine,' swooned Romilda, gazing across the road at the red-faced Jürgen, who was already wrapped in an embrace with another woman.

The Boa Viagem girls all shared the same illusions. They all claimed that they were not really prostitutes, preferring some more accept-able word; and they all clung to the dream that one day a foreigner might fall in love with them. Like poverty-stricken gamblers hoping desperately that the lottery would prove their escape ticket from misery, the girls looked at every new punter in the hope that this might turn out to be the one they had hoped for, the one who would fall in love with a pretty dark-skinned teenager. The Brazilians call them 'Summertime Cinderellas' – though most, like Romilda, are cruelly betrayed in their choice of prince.

As for the foreigners, love was the last thing on their minds. I talked to a German at one of the bar tables. He was clutching a skinny black girl on his lap – his tenth girl that week, he boasted. 'Don't blame me, I'm doing her a favour,' he crowed. 'If she weren't sleeping with me she'd be sleeping on a shanty floor with her ten cousins. She's lucky I picked her.'

Midnight, and the craft fair was reduced to a few stands selling roasted meat spits or filled samosas, and the iron skeletons of other stalls that had closed. The white church sat eerily lit from below, illuminating a blue police cabin next door. The bars were busier than ever, taxis were doing good business, and the music was playing at full volume, drowning out the noisy chatter of German, English and pidgin-Portuguese. I began to think about leaving.

As I was about to get up, another girl arrived, hobbling clumsily on stilt-like heels. She was a tiny girl, dressed in a black leotard and skimpy shorts, her face caked in make-up. He lips were a crimson slash; her eyes were thickly outlined in black.

'Hey everybody, I'm back!' She included the whole square in her raucous greeting. 'I've run away from Febem! I've escaped!' Febem was the state orphanage.

When she saw Romilda the girl squealed and rushed to greet her. While they were talking animatedly, another thickly-moustached German called the new girl over and asked how much she charged.

'Fifty *reals* for five hours,' she replied. 'But I won't do it unless Romilda comes with me.'

The German went back to his beer in a huff. There was no shortage of young girls offering themselves for less. He could afford to wait until a cheaper, less demanding specimen passed by.

Later I talked to her. Her name was Maria Luisa. She was twelve years old. She was reluctant to talk about herself and declined to discuss her family. Her body was tiny and undeveloped, the body of a child.

'How can you manage five hours?' I asked. 'Most of the tourists around here seem overweight.'

'It hurts. I put up with it,' she said tersely. 'I need the money.'

I stayed in Boa Viagem for a fortnight and got to know many of the Brazilians who lived on and around the square. Many of them depended on the sex trade for their living: bar-owners, stall-keepers, hotel porters, taxi-drivers and many more.

One night I was walking along the beach back to my hotel.

'Matt!' – It was José, the coconut kiosk owner whose skills had impressed me on New Year's morning. I had got to know him quite well.

'Yes?'

'I'm after a rat,' he panted. 'I nearly got it but it ran under this car. It won't come out and I can't get at it. Here, you hold this – '

He handed me a flip-flop. 'Wait by the car here and I'll try to hit it with my catapult. When it runs out you hit it with the shoe. OK?'

To the amusement of passers-by, he dropped on to his hands and knees and aimed sideways underneath the car with a lethal-looking catapult. He fired. There was a strangled squeal. A rat the size of my foot scrambled out from under the car and I duly thwacked it with the flip-flop. The poor creature limped to a standstill and the bystanders burst into approving applause. José, with evident enthusiasm, finished the rat off with a brick.

Roberval was a tourist guide. He had worked the Boa Viagem beachfront for almost twenty years. He was known as *Secador* – 'the man who lets down car tyres'. According to Roberval, a foreigner had once offered him 100 *reals* to puncture the tyres of a fellow-foreigner. 'Twenty five *reals* per tyre – who wouldn't have done it? And from then on everyone on the square started calling me the *Secador*.'

According to Roberval, the word on the square was, 'The dollar speaks loudest of all.' If you had money you could do whatever you wanted, whether it was letting down someone's tyres or having sex with a child. 'The police don't stop the *gringos*,' he explained. 'The only time they stop is when their money runs out.'

Though he called himself a tour guide, he was really a middleman. He patrolled the beach looking for tourists to whom he could sell accommodation in one of the blocks of self-contained flats by the square – blocks like the Holliday, a scruffy crescent-shaped high-rise behind the main hotel strip, from the windows of which a number of German and Italian flags were draped.

'The *gringos* like to change their girls like they change their shirts,' laughed Roberval. Some of them never left their rooms, even to go to the beach. Roberval collected girls for them to order, and delivered them to the tourists' rooms. 'They tell me what type, how old – and I go and find them. Just like a shopping list!'

I asked him how many girls such men would get through in one week.

'Oh, I can't keep count. One in the morning ... another in the afternoon ... sometimes more.' He rubbed his thumb and forefinger together, the universal symbol. 'That's what speaks loudest, you see.'

Roberval had his own moral code. 'Not all tour guides are fair,' he smirked. 'There are some real swindlers. Sometimes they put sleeping pills in the *gringos'* drinks and rob them of everything they have! The *gringos* end up so skint, they have to ask us to sell their clothes to raise money! Naturally, *I* would never do such a thing.' He dug his hand in his pocket and, winking elaborately, casually produced a bottle of sleeping pills.

Roberval was a fund of information. 'Some of
the *gringos* are just as unscrupulous. They ask
the girls to marry them, then take them back to
Europe and make them work for them as sex
slaves. Some escape and manage to get back to
Brazil but most are too ashamed to say what
really happened.'

'Do you think one of those girls would be
willing to talk to me?'

Roberval considered. 'I'll ask around and get
back to you. But I will want something from
you in exchange. A souvenir from England!'

Two days later, Roberval told me that he had
found a seventeen-year-old girl who was prepared to talk to me. Her name was Ana Lúcia.
She had been held prisoner in Germany but had
managed to escape. Recently she had managed
to get back to Brazil.

My meeting with Ana Lúcia cost me my
'England 5, Germany 1' T-shirt. She was a beautiful girl, softly-spoken and articulate. We sat
on a concrete bench behind the church, away
from the noise of the main street.

'It's painful for me to remember what
happened,' she said.

'I know. Tell me how you began as a prostitute,' I suggested.

'I was fifteen, my mother was poor, we did-
n't have enough to eat. What could I do? What
does anybody do? My mother had no money
for food. So I had to start selling my body to the

gringos. That was how I met Kristian. He asked me to go to Germany with him. I said "Yes". I'm a prostitute – but I fall in love too, you know. Anyway, my aunt lives in Germany.'

When Ana Lúcia arrived at Stuttgart Airport, Kristian and two other men met her. 'I knew something wasn't right, and I began to feel scared. They drove me to a flat and locked me in a tiny room. There was just a bed, no other furniture. I cried and cried ... I was locked up there for over a month.'

She had become the victim of a systematic-ally planned kidnap. 'He only opened the door to give me food – and to let the men in. He made me sleep with lots of men. Of course he kept all the money. I used to cry and scream, begging him to let me go back to Brazil, but he just told me, "You aren't going back for a long, long time." He said he was going to sell me to another man for $1,000.'

'How did you manage to get back to Brazil?'

'He forgot to lock the door one day, and I escaped. I rang my aunt and she paid for my ticket home.'

Ana's appalling story is not exceptional. Hundreds of girls like her are duped into going abroad by promises of marriage or work. Many of those who go never come back. When later I spoke to Recife's police chief, Olga Câmara, I learned that according to police figures five

thousand women and girls are trafficked
abroad every year. An estimated seventy-five
thousand Brazilian women are being held as
sex slaves in European brothels, mostly in
Germany, Spain, Portugal and Italy.

Once, Recife was the centre of the Brazilian
slave trade. More than one hundred years after
the abolition of slavery, very little seems to have
changed. At Boa Viagem dark-skinned girls are
bought and sold on the marketplace, taken
from their homes and locked up in foreign
countries. And the people who are operating
this immensely profitable trade are white
Europeans.

The fifteenth of January was my last day in
Recife, and my birthday. I was now twenty-
eight, a fact that I naturally did my best to
forget as I strolled down to the Boa Viagem
square for the last time.

As always, the place was teeming with
teenagers, parading in front of the white men
sitting around the beer-bottle-cluttered tables.
Tonight, more than ever, I felt sickened and
angry. Police strolled round the square in pairs,
or sat inside their blue cabin, watching noncha-
lantly as the foreigners blatantly broke the law.
If it were enforced, such men could expect a
prison sentence of up to four years, or at least
a hefty fine and deportation. In the International Airport at Recife government posters

were displayed: two piercing eyes and the words 'Brazil is watching you'. And so Brazil was: but watching seemed to be just about all Brazil was doing.

Romilda was already cruising the bar tables. When she saw me, she dashed into one of the bars and emerged carrying a plastic bag.

'Happy birthday! Here's your present.'

I was overwhelmed. I could not even remember telling her about my birthday. I looked inside the bag. Inside was a blue cap, embroidered with the letter 'R'. 'It's so you don't forget about me,' she said. 'I want you to tell people about my life.'

I thanked her and promised that I would always remember her. I told her I would be leaving next morning, and she wept. Then, wiping her tears away, she crossed the road and returned to the tables and the drinking foreigners.

Amanda and Juliana were two ten-year-olds who were always on the square. They would mill around the fair stalls or go into the bars and restaurants, selling boiled sweets or asking for spare change. Small and cute, they had no problem persuading people to part with their loose coins.

Late on my last night, little Amanda appeared on the square as usual. But tonight she was different. She was not barefoot, and the shoebox full of sweets was nowhere to be seen. The tiny girl was dressed in a silky dress, her hair tied back in a ribbon. She was walking arm-in-arm with an older girl.

I watched in horror as the older girl paraded Amanda in front of the seated foreigners, like a showman exhibiting a choice young heifer at a cattle market. One of the tourists showed a keen interest in her and started what were obviously negotiations.

I could not bear to stand watching. Furious, I marched over and crashed my fist down on to the metal table. Beer spilled out of his tankard.

'What do you think you're doing?' I raged.

He looked at me blankly – not with anger particularly, but seemingly with real perplexity. 'What's the problem?'

'Do you realise how old this girl is?'

He laughed. 'So what? Go on then, call the police. They're over there, see?'

I stormed over to the blue police cabin and entered without knocking. Inside, an inspector was lounging, watching football on a portable TV.

'Have you any idea what's going on out there? A ten-year-old child is being sold to the tourists!'

He waved me towards the door, not unkindly. 'There's nothing I can do, you see, *senhor*. My job here is to protect the tourists. I can do nothing about this child. You see my problem, I'm certain…' His soothing excuses followed me as I stumbled back out into the warm crowded square, the baroque church rising severe and faceless into the night, the bars and clubs echoing with the Babel of languages of those who had come to buy a young girl for the night.

I strode back to my hotel shaking with anger. I slammed the door of my room shut and flung myself down on my bed, weeping bitterly. I knew that God's heart was breaking for the poor, used, broken young girls of Recife.

I was still carrying Romilda's birthday gift in my hand. Still gulping back tears, I clutched the blue cap with its beautifully embroidered 'R'.

'No, I won't forget you,' I vowed. 'I won't forget any of you.'

7

The Sertão: Impossible Choices

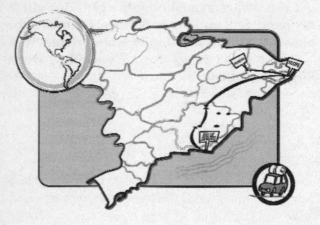

The north-eastern region of Brazil, in which Recife is located, was the first part of the country to be developed economically: slave plantations in the tropical coastal plains made it a major sugar-cane producing region. Today the North-East is still a major agricultural region, and its main cities – Salvador, Fortaleza, and Recife – are each home to more than a million people.

Three hundred miles inland from this fertile coast, occupying the north-western tip of Pernambuco State, lies Brazil's most arid region, the Sertão. Punished by perpetual drought and periodic famine, its 43 million people struggle to survive in crippling poverty. Malnutrition, infant mortality and illiteracy are sky high.

I was not surprised to learn that the Sertão has a high incidence of child prostitution. My information came from Cristiano Jerônimo, a journalist from the *Diário de Pernambuco* newspaper in Recife. He suggested that I visit an area known as the 'Triangle of Prostitution', fifty square miles bounded by three of the Sertão's main towns – Ouricuri, Trinidade and Araripina. There, Cristiano told me, thousands of young girls were selling their bodies, and it was even known for mothers and fathers to sell their own children. I decided to hire a car and drive to Araripina, leave it there and continue north.

I left Recife at dawn. I was not sure how long the journey would take; I was in trouble as soon as I drove out of the car-hire shop and turned thoughtlessly left onto a one-way street going right. My problems multiplied over the next two hours as I tried frantically to negotiate Recife's chaotic roads, bridges, four-lane flyovers, spiralling access lanes and narrow one-way streets. It was the height of the morning rush hour. By the time I found the motorway I was already far behind schedule.

The straight road ahead of me rose and fell for mile after mile. As I conquered each crest another was revealed further on, blurred by a weary haze of heat. The landscape became more and more inhospitable, barren and lifeless. Tall spiny cacti clung to the dusty soil.

The road crossed a number of wooden bridges, each of them with a sign showing the name of the river over which it passed. But there was not even a trickle of water in the lifeless channels; just dried-up silt cracked by the searing heat. This region had seen no rain for almost ten years.

The roadside was dotted with many tiny stone grottos, in front of which wooden crucifixes or wilting posies were laid. My first thought was that they were shrines to the many different images of Mary that are worshipped in Brazil, such as 'Our Lady of Good Advice', 'Our Lady of an Easy Birth', or the curious 'Our Lady of Oh' – I often wondered when it was appropriate to pray to her. I stopped at one of the shrines to have a closer look and found that they were actually memorials to people who had been killed. I wondered how so many people could have died on such a straight, almost empty road. I later discovered that most of the unfortunate drivers had collided not with other cars but with donkeys, cows and horses.

I had a few near-misses of my own. The horses and cows, I noticed, would cross from one side of the road to the other. The donkeys, however, just stood in the middle of the road looking perplexed, as if it was *I* blocking *their* path. Sometimes the traffic would be brought to a complete halt as a stubborn donkey had a staring match with an articulated lorry. No wonder the Brazilian word for 'stupid' also means 'donkey'. I pressed on. As I crossed the busy BR-116 motorway, heavy black clouds in the afternoon sky were threatening rain.

By the time I finally arrived in Araripina, nearly twelve hours after leaving Boa Viagem seafront, torrential rain was drumming on the roof of my car. The rains seemed to have brought the entire town out onto the streets. Soaked children, shouting and squealing, danced beneath water spouting from drainage pipes, or in torrents gushing down gutters in the road. Some of them had not seen rain in their entire lives; most had had no running water in their homes for years.

I checked in to the only hotel in town.

'We English always bring the bad weather with us!' I joked.

The receptionist looked blank. It was not that she did not understand the joke. She simply could not understand why I had called the rain 'bad'.

Next morning the rain had become a steady downpour. As I strolled out of the hotel I made a point of commenting how good the weather was, and this time got a smile in return. No wonder: during the last famine nine million people had been driven to the brink of starvation, and many hundreds died. The child mortality rate had doubled to 425 deaths for every thousand live births. A third of all deaths were caused by diarrhoea, the result of drinking dirty water. When things were at their worst, families had resorted to eating cacti, the only crop that had survived.

Araripina was a typical outback town. Men wearing straw hats and frayed cotton trousers sauntered along the muddy streets. Women balanced bulging sacks or woven baskets on their heads. Pigs and chickens roamed around the town centre streets, while Brahman bulls meandered purposefully in alleyways. In normal dry weather it must have been a dusty place – five hundred lorries a day come to Araripina, destined for the open-cast quarries in the surrounding hills, where thousands of tonnes of gypsum are carved out for use in making plaster of Paris and in the building industry. I wondered how the town could be so poor, with such a thriving local industry.

Out of sheer curiosity, I decided to visit a gypsum quarry. The receptionist at the hotel gave me directions to one that lay at the end of a dirt track on the outskirts of the town. It was owned by a French company, Lafarge, and was one of the largest gypsum plants in the area.

The plant manager was a young man called Alexandre. He offered to give me a tour of the site, which, he explained, extracted one hundred thousand tonnes of gypsum every month. Lafarge owned mines in seventy-five countries and made twelve billion euro in sales every year. Ninety-five per cent of Brazil's entire production of gypsum stone, Alexandre told me, comes from the Araripina region – giving the area the national nickname of 'The Plaster Pole'.

Wearing a hard hat, I toured the main plant and watched a huge machine crushing white rocks to fine powder. Massive metal furnaces purified the powder with blasts of intense heat. A lone operator was in charge of the machine. 'The whole process is automated,' commented Alexandre. 'So it is very labour-saving.'

'Do you employ local people?'

'A handful.'

Outside, lorries waited to collect their cargoes. Most were from the southern industrial states: Rio de Janeiro, São Paula, Paraná; some had come from Florianópolis and Porto Alegre, nearly two thousand miles away. The trucks would wait in Araripina for two or three days while their consignment was loaded, then make the long journey back.

The Plaster Pole comprised Ouricuri, Trinidade and Araripina – the very same towns that comprised the Triangle of Prostitution. It was no coincidence.

'In Trinidade, it's estimated that twelve per cent of the town's teenagers are caught up in the sex trade,' I was told by Silviano Neto of the Pernambuco State Children's Council. 'In Araripina it is far worse. Girls as young as eight years old sell their bodies for as little as one real.' A real is, in British currency, about thirty pence. 'When evening comes,' Silviano told me, 'the prostitution points are crowded with truck drivers waiting for the children to arrive.'

That night I climbed the steep cobbled hill from my hotel in Araripina to the *Petrobrás* petrol station on the main highway. I wanted to speak to some of the truck drivers who were staying in the town overnight while they waited for their lorries to be loaded.

I had only just arrived when a loud-mouthed truck driver started talking to me. He announced himself as Armando from Campinas, near São Paulo. He was scruffy and unshaven, wearing a string vest over a bulging beer-belly. As he spoke he swigged from a can of beer in one hand and a glass of

pinga rum in the other. His speech was full of
obscenities.

'I've been collecting gypsum from Araripina
for fourteen years. It goes down south for a
building firm.' He winked at me balefully. 'If
my wife knew what I get up to on the road
she'd leave me. Or kill me,' he laughed.

The banter moved from women to sex to *quen-
gas*, the north-eastern nickname for prostitutes.
'These little girls, they're just vermin – *vagabundas*,'
he snorted. 'Once a friend of mine was caught red-
handed with one in the back of his cab. He had to
pay a 2,500 *real* fine and was grounded here for
four days. He came back later, found the girl and
killed her.' Armando took a long swig of rum, as if
toasting his angry friend.

'When a little *quenga* knocks on my cab door
I say, "Sure! Let's do it." Then when she's inside
I slam the door shut and go speeding off right
into the middle of the bush. Just to teach her a
lesson. Then I kick the whore out, right there in
the middle of nowhere! Ha!' He took another
swig and belched, loudly and self-righteously.
By now other drinking partners had sat down
beside him, joining in the banter.

'I must have made about fifteen of the little
bitches pregnant!' he roared, and the others
roared back in approving laughter.

I slipped away. I was nauseated and angry.
I remembered little Leidiane, the '1.99 girl',
who was carrying a truck driver's baby.

Armando's route back to Campinas would take him through Governador Valadares where Leidiane lived. I might have just been talking to the foul-mouthed slob who had fathered her child.

Later I talked to one of the young girls on the petrol station forecourt. Twelve-year-old Janice was going from lorry to lorry, knocking on cab doors. Small and bony, she wore polka-dot shorts and carried a rucksack in the shape of a fluffy teddy bear over one shoulder. I asked her how much she charged.

'Four *reals*. I'm more expensive than the others because I look younger. I'm small and I've got a flat chest. The men like that better, I don't know why.'

'What do you spend the money on?'

'Stupid things – clothes, sometimes. And I always give some to my parents.'

'They know you're here?'

'Yeah.'

'And they don't mind?'

'Oh, sure! Mum says she's ashamed to have a daughter who's a *quenga*. She cries all the time. I feel so bad when I see my mum crying, or praying to Our Lady of Oh.'

Janice leaned against the huge wheel of an HGV. It dwarfed her. 'I think I'm going to leave this way of life,' she said. 'I can't keep living like this. I don't think I'll come here again, after tonight.'

The little girl wandered off through the parked lorries, disappearing into a cloud of exhaust fumes.

The rain continued remorselessly on. It rained for four days, sometimes a light drizzle, sometimes a deluge. Nobody could remember when it had last rained so heavily. Certainly the region's main crops – corn, sweet potato and manioc – would not fail this year. And the rain had damped down the insufferable heat.

However, the rain did not bring only good news. Many rivers burst their banks, flooding roads and sweeping away the tiny mud-brick houses. In one nearby village two people died when their cottage collapsed on top of them. In the Jequitinhonha Valley, some six hundred miles away, freak rainfall was also wreaking havoc. Thirty people died in a mudslide that flattened a row of houses in Araçuaí, where I had stayed for a night. I remember the frail old lady to whom I had given a lift. She had been praying desperately for rain so that she would not die of thirst. Now even the rain was killing people.

It was late afternoon, and I was on the back of an open-top lorry bumping and jolting along a narrow twisting road. With me was Márcia Araújo, a social worker from Araripina's Town Council. She was responsible for the town's PETI programme, a federal government scheme aimed at combating child labour. She also co-ordinated a campaign against child prostitution in the town and ran a self-help group for more than a hundred teenage girls involved in the sex trade. Many of them lived in Marcolândia, a tiny rural village on the border with the neighbouring state of Piauí.

There are no buses to Marcolândia – hence the lorry. It was covered with tarpaulin and crammed with people: their clothes shabby, their faces worn and rugged. Some of the women carried babies in their arms, while the men carried bulging hessian sacks or bunches of chicken tied together by their legs. One had a pig strapped to his back. As we bumped along they chatted happily, but their north-eastern dialect was almost impossible to understand. They would shorten some words, or run whole sentences into a few blurred syllables punctuated with plentiful 'Aaah!'s and 'Eer!'s. I could not make out a single word.

The lorry reached the motorway border post in Marcolândia. We all climbed down: lorries had to have their loads weighed at the border and state taxes had to be paid before they were allowed to cross. Drivers, explained Márcia, often stayed overnight in Marcolândia, while their loads and documents were inspected.

Behind the border post there was a village of tiny terraced cottages. The sandy road squelched underfoot as we made our way around the large pools of rainwater. A few bare toddlers splashed excitedly in the puddles.

Among the mud-brick houses were many small factories producing *farinha*, a coarse flour made from the manioc root, a traditional accompaniment to the Brazilian meal of rice and beans. 'There are only two ways for people in Marcolândia to make money,' observed Márcia. 'Scraping the skin off manioc, or selling sex to strangers at the border post.'

She took me to visit a number of families whose daughters took part in her self-help group. Their homes were desperately poor, often just a single room with dirt floors and walls of mud mixed with straw. In our conversations nobody mentioned what their daughters did after nightfall. 'In a close-knit community like this,' Márcia told me, 'nobody will admit that their daughter is a *quenga*.' Even so, many families were dependent on their daughters' income.

'You can only get work in the *farinha* factories,' one mother told us. 'But the pay is nothing. When the drought comes, what you get for skinning manioc for a whole day isn't even enough to buy a litre of water.'

As Márcia and I stood talking on the roadside a young girl hurried by, clutching a sharp knife. Her name was Adeidiane, she was eleven years old, and she was covered in white dust. She was on her way home after working in a *farinha* factory.

'How much do you earn there?' I asked her.

'I get 60 *centavos* for every basket of manioc I skin. But I only did two baskets today.'

Adeidiane told me that she started work at five o'clock in the morning. It was now five o'clock in the afternoon. This eleven-year-old worked a gruelling twelve-hour day, and earned just one real and 20 *centavos* – the equivalent of around 35 pence.

The young girl's hands were roughened and covered in small scars. As she talked she coughed and wheezed, and complained of chest pains. Even so, she was eager to get back home. She was due to play football with her friends on the dirt track in front of her house.

'Can I go to the factory with you tomorrow?' I asked.

'If you want to. Meet me at my house, it's over there. Five o'clock I start out.'

It was still dark when I arrived at Adeidiane's house. I had staggered out of bed at 4 am, taken a taxi to Marcolândia and walked the short distance from the motorway to our arranged meeting point. Adeidiane emerged, tired-eyed, from her cottage. We walked for a short distance across a manioc field towards the *farinha* factory.

'I didn't want to get up this morning.' She yawned. 'I was really tired. I ached all over. I just wanted to stay in bed.'

'What about school?'

'Oh, I dream about going to school! I love to write and draw. I asked my mother to enrol me in school for next term. But I don't know if I'll be able to.'

'Why not?'

'I have to work to help my family. My mum washes clothes, but there's hardly ever any water. She doesn't force me to work. But if I didn't, there wouldn't be any food for me and my brothers.'

When we arrived, the factory was already fully operational. Most of the workers were women, but some were girls of Adeidiane's age or younger. They were already hard at work among piles of brown manioc root. The factory interior was hot and thick with dust. Two stone mills crushed the skinned root, grinding it to a coarse flour which was then roasted on another large rotating stone heated by a furnace. Adeidiane squatted down on the dirt floor beside her basket and began skinning a manioc with her knife.

'I've got to work hard today,' she smiled. 'I've got to finish three baskets.' The baskets were enormous, twice as big as laundry baskets. Adeidiane's tiny hands could not keep up with the other women working around her.

As her small fingers worked the tough skin from the root, she told me about her twelve-year-old friend, Selma, who had worked at the same factory for the same wage, until a year previously.

'Then she started selling her body at the border post. She charges ten *reals* a time. Ten *reals*! That's more than I get a week. But I wouldn't have the courage to do that.'

'You've got more courage than you think,' I assured her. I stayed for a while longer before saying goodbye and walking back through the manioc field towards the border post. I planned to try to catch a lorry back to Araripina; from there I would take a bus to the coastal city of Fortaleza, five hundred miles further north.

Walking over the field, I looked at the green manioc leaves sprouting from under the waterlogged soil. In the distance I could hear the faint boom of gypsum being blasted out of the hills. I thought of little Adeidiane, diligently skinning her manioc to keep her family from starving. Meanwhile, foreign companies were making millions.

Brazil is the world's eighth largest economic power, with a GDP of $789 billion. Every year it attracts $30 billion of foreign investment. Yet fifty-three million people live in poverty, and twenty-three million in abject misery. Half of those live at the Plaster Pole – one of Brazil's richest areas, measured in terms of natural resources.

As much as I try to do the sums, it never seems to add up.

It is always children who bear the brunt of Brazil's unjust society. Girls like Adeidiane, with her scarred and roughened hands and troubling chest pains, are forced to choose between twelve hours of back-breaking work in a sweatshop, and selling her young body on the streets. It is a choice no eleven-year-old should ever have to make.

Fortaleza: 'I'm not a whore, I'm just a little girl'

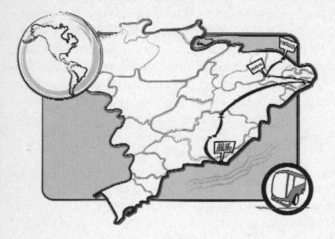

In Fortaleza, pizza is sold by the metre. I ordered 22 centimetres of Margherita and a Coca-cola. After two weeks in the Sertão it was good to be eating European food again. In Araripina there had been little else other than rice, beans and the ubiquitous *farinha*. The regional delicacy there was roast goat, and the vegetarian option, a dish called *baião de dois* – whose recipe I estimated to be rice mixed with beans, accompanied by *farinha*. It was also sheer bliss to be able to take a bite without getting a mouthful of flies.

In that strange mixture of wealth and poverty that characterises so much of modern Brazil, Fortaleza boasts an impressive development of bars and restaurants overlooking the sea. The beach and the sea itself are illuminated at night by floodlights, and a paved promenade stretches for two miles linking two popular beach resorts, Iracema and Beira-Mar. I was sitting in a gleaming pizzeria in the new development, near a metal lantern-hung structure that jutted out to sea. The locals call it the Bridge of the English, presumably because it is actually a pier, the only one in Brazil. They obviously could not call it a pier, which in Portuguese means 'sink'.

The pizza was square, authentic and delicious. And so it should have been: the restaurant was owned by an Italian immigrant. Most of the diners were Italian – a good sign. The only Brazilians in the place seemed to be my dinner guests, Luizianne Lins – a prominent city councillor who was running for state governor – and Nágela, her PA.

Luizianne was chairing an extensive parliamentary enquiry into sex tourism in Fortaleza – an enquiry launched at her instigation. 'We discovered that a tour company had published a brochure in Italy offering a seven-day package holiday here in Fortaleza. In it they promised young Brazilian girls for $25 each.'

She bit into her pizza and carried on talking. 'We watched CCTV footage taken from the arrivals lounge at the airport. The same guides were always there to meet the Milan flight. They always came with the same group of girls. Everybody seemed to know everybody else. We were sure something sinister was going on.'

Over four months Luizianne interviewed more than sixty people: hoteliers, tour operators, policemen, taxi drivers, restaurant owners, local residents, and the girls themselves. Because it was a government enquiry, those called upon to testify were obliged to do so. The findings were far more disturbing than anybody had expected. A network of Italians was controlling the prostitution of children with foreigners in Fortaleza. The group owned many of the resort's hotels, tourist apartments and guest houses.

Luizianne's findings pointed even further: the group was behind a much larger network, drawing in local taxi drivers, beach hut owners and the proprietors of restaurants and nightclubs. The girls, some as young as seven and eight years old, were recruited from nearby *favela* shanty towns. The taxi drivers collected them from their homes and delivered them to the flat or hotel where the foreigner was staying. Because most of the tourist accommodation in Fortaleza was owned by members of the group, there was almost no chance of being caught. The whole scheme was virtually watertight.

Luizianne slipped me a file that included profiles of some of these local godfathers, and their photos.

One man owned nineteen apartments, each of them worth $50,000. His apartment blocks on the Beira-Mar seafront were safe havens for Italian sex tourists. He had already been sentenced to three years' imprisonment for involvement in child prostitution, but the sentence had been overturned on appeal. He was also cited in a recent investigation into a powerful drugs cartel that operated in Fortaleza.

Another man was one of those who met the Italian tourists at the airport and took them to the hotels and apartments owned by other Italians in the ring. He was also known to recruit young girls in nightclubs and to take lewd photographs of girls for distribution on the internet. Charges of drug smuggling had also been made against him.

I turned the pages of the file and looked at the photographs of these and other handsome, corrupt foreigners who were prepared to destroy the lives of another nation's children for the sake of immense personal gain. One of

the reasons I had come back to Brazil was to
find out how deeply the corruption was
ingrained into Brazilian society. Now I was in
shock. I had never imagined that child prostitution could be so well organised and that such
huge sums of money could be involved – sums
all the more obscene when one considered the
utter poverty of the *favela* girls being exploited.
Between the millionaires living in splendour in
Milan, and little Adeidiane in the Sertão –
working a twelve- hour day for 35 pence, trying
to stave off the day when she too would make
the journey up to the motorway to keep her
family from starvation – there was a direct and
documented connection.

I closed the file and handed it back. 'You
must be at some considerable personal risk, as
head of the committee. Are you worried that
you might become a target?'

'I've had several death threats,' Luizianne
replied calmly. 'But the indignation I feel is
greater than the fear. That's why I haven't given
up.'

I later read Luizianne's full report, signed by
six other councillors in the city and presented to
the Fortaleza City Council and the Senate in
Brasília. It called for a number of urgent meas-
ures, including the arrest of the Italians and
others involved in the prostitution rings.
Luizianne's indignation sounded loud and
clear in the report's conclusions. She spoke of

'the ironic and perverse meeting of two worlds'
on the beachfront of Fortaleza:

> The tourists, convinced that they can do anything
> they like, have no qualms about buying the
> sexual favours of children. The girls, crushed by
> misery, family breakdown and the absence or fail-
> ure of public policies for the poor, see sex tourism
> as a way out of abject misery, a door to things and
> places unimaginable for someone of their social
> standing.

My dinner with Luizianne and Nágela had
given me some valuable information – and an
enormous credit card bill. Twenty-two centimetres of Italian dough had cost more than my
entire week's consumption of rice and beans in
the Sertão. I mulled over both the information
and the bill as I strolled along the promenade,
following the curve of the beach towards Beira-
Mar where the city's luxury hotels were located.
Luizianne's comment about her indignation
being greater than her fear stuck in my memory.
It was to inspire me many times during the
remainder of my journey.

The promenade was crowded with people
walking, jogging or rollerblading. Stalls were
selling popcorn, cashew nuts or tapioca cakes
filled with cheese. Some promenaders had
stopped to watch an impromptu performance by
a juggling clown, a fire-breather, or a comedy

duo singing songs of the region and telling dirty jokes. One man, sprayed silver, stood like a statue in the middle of the promenade surrounded by a crowd of curious onlookers.

The Beira-Mar beachfront was a colourful and vibrant crescent bordered by high-rise hotels and packed with people. Many were *fortalezenses* mingling with the tourists and selling hand-made craftwork, dyed sarongs, Brazilian football shirts and pencil portraits of Pelé and Leonardo di Caprio. Others had found creative ways of taking the tourists' money without selling them anything. An old bag lady shuffled along the promenade with a two-litre Coca-cola bottle balanced on her head, filled with water and a red rose.

I looked at high-rise hotels in Fortaleza differently, now that I had read Luizianne's report. They were the visible front of a hidden international web of child prostitution, and the location where much of it took place. In the same way, I looked at the taxis drawn up alongside a busy McDonald's and remembered the report's claim that many taxi drivers on the Beira-Mar were linked with the Italian mafia.

I decided to put the claim to the test. I opened the door of the first taxi in the queue and got in. '*Pousada Araras*,' I said, naming a guesthouse I had passed in the bus on the way to the pizzeria.

The driver swivelled round and nodded. He had a whiskery face above a pointed chin.

He wore a huge silver medallion on his hairy chest and his expression was inscrutable through reflective mirror sunglasses. He counted fifteen on his fingers, and I gave him a thumbs-up – I knew I was being ripped off, the guesthouse was only five minutes' drive away, but I did not want to blow my cover as an Italian tourist by arguing about the fare.

For an Englishman, speaking broken Portuguese with an Italian accent is more difficult than it sounds. As we neared the guesthouse I cleared my thoat.

'Er … *Você conhece … bambitas*?'

'Oh – you mean girls.'

'*Sim.*'

'You want me to bring a girl here?'

'*Sim … Bem novinha*?'

'Yeah? *How* young?'

I counted out 'fifteen' on my fingers, then gestured 'more or less'.

'No problem,' he grinned. 'Fifty for her; thirty for me. OK?'

He gave me the thumbs-up and drove off.

I did not hang around to see if the taxi driver would return with the girl. I wrote down his name and number plate and eventually passed the information on to Luizianne. It was duly included in her complete report, as was the other information I collected in Fortaleza. The taxi driver's name, with that of the fleet owner, was passed on to the Juvenile Police Unit.

The driver's total lack of surprise at my request, and his readiness to fulfil it, indicated that what I had already seen of Luizianne's report was accurate. The other information in that report made me hope that I did not meet up with that particular taxi driver again. And I certainly had no wish to meet his employers.

Next day I held on tight as the bus bumped and swerved along a busy main street behind Beira-Mar seafront. I was going to Serviluz, a large *favela* shanty town where the Beira-Mar taxi drivers went to pick up girls (and where last night's taxi-driver had probably gone). The slum began where Beira-Mar's chic boulevards and fast-food restaurants ended; the high-rise apartments and five-star hotels gave way abruptly to an untidy mish-mash of brick shacks and corrugated iron roofs.

In Serviluz, Peter and Selma Thomas were beginning a new project under the auspices of Youth With A Mission (YWAM), a Christian organisation working with children in a number of Brazilian cities. Peter was waiting to meet me as the bus jolted to a halt outside a scruffy roadside bar in the shadow of a disused lighthouse.

I had not met Peter before. He had written to me after reading *Street Girls*, telling me that he and his Brazilian wife were about to move to the slums of Serviluz to begin an outreach to the *favela* children. When I first arrived in

Fortaleza, long before I read Luizianne's report and learned of the slum's prostitution problem, I rang him, eager to know how the new project was progressing.

'We didn't know how many girls were involved in prostitution,' said Peter as we walked up a steep hill to their house. 'It was only when we got here and lived among them that we realised how bad the problem was.'

As we walked, Peter told me how God had called him and his wife to Serviluz. 'We rented a house right here in the slum and began to get to know the families. We started to find that many of the girls were prostitutes – all from broken, difficult homes.'

He told me about Marta. She was seven years old. Marta roamed round the narrow alleyways of the *favela* begging for scraps of food. Her mother was a drug addict and worried more about her next fix than her daughter's well being. 'Every couple of weeks a posh car with blacked-out windows comes here and picks up Marta. I've seen it myself. She's gone for two or three days, then she's dropped back here. Her mother doesn't even notice she's gone.'

Peter knew of other young girls involved in the Italian-controlled prostitution rings. Some had confided in him and Selma: girls like thirteen-year-old Michele, who sometimes waited for the taxi drivers on the main street with her fourteen-year-old friend Tatiane.

We reached the top of the hill and were rewarded with a dramatic view. Across the landscape sprawled the *favela*'s red-brick towers; beyond, Beira-Mar's glass-gilded skyscrapers soared into the sky. Below us, huge waves crashed noisily in a small bay. It was called Titanzinho Bay, explained Peter, and was one of the best surfing spots in Brazil. Tita Tavares, the current world women's surfing champion, had grown up in the *favela*, 'She is one of the lucky ones. Most the girls who grow up here have very little chance of making anything of their lives.'

Most of the children, he said, came from broken homes. It was very rare to find a mother and father who stayed together. 'The kids are used to seeing their mothers swapping partners. Most don't even know who their fathers are. Many of the girls have been sexually abused by their mother's partner or by other males in the family. And the *favela* families often sleep in the same room. The children grow up seeing and hearing adult things. The average age at which a girl loses her virginity is eleven.'

The mission of Peter and Selma seemed daunting beyond belief. Ten thousand people lived in the *favela*; violence was part of everyday life there and drug abuse was widespread. But the couple were determined to make a difference, and their love for the children they had come to help was evident.

Later Peter took me to visit Michele, the thirteen-year-old who waited for the taxi drivers with her friend Tatiane.

She lived in the ground floor of a two-storey brick building on a dusty road further down the hill. The door was opened by Michele's mother, a baby balanced on her hip. Inside was a wooden bed with a dirty foam mattress, and a flickering TV. Two young children were playing on the dirt floor.

'I haven't seen Michele for three days. She left on Tuesday – she said she was going to a party or something. It's been like this since she was nine. She just disappears for days on end, Sometimes she's gone for weeks.'

As we left I asked her to let Peter know if Michele turned up.

'Sure. But don't get your hopes up. I wouldn't be surprised if I never saw my daughter again.'

As we made our way back Peter told me how Michele's fifteen-year-old brother was himself a prostitute on Beira-Mar. Her older sister Adriana was currently serving a two-year sentence for pimping under-age girls. What hope did Michele have of a different life?

Peter and Selma were convinced there *was* hope. And they were determined to bring it to the poor girls of Serviluz.

Every road in the run-down area of Barra do Ceará looked the same, and there were no street signs. My taxi driver had been driving for over half an hour round and round the same few square miles. He claimed not to know the area: I didn't believe him. This was one of the main night-time destinations with over sixty motels crammed into a few blocks.

By the time we finally found 1142 Assis Street, the taxi meter had clocked up 25 *reals* and 80 *centavos*. The driver had watched the numbers increasing with every sign of satisfaction. As we stopped, the dial gave one last jump to 26.

He glanced at the meter and pulled out a card from underneath the sun visor.

'Let's see ... 26 *reals*. That's be 34 *reals*, then.'

'What?'

'It's the new tariff. They haven't changed all the meters yet. So that's 34 *reals*.'

I was beginning to wish I were back in the Sertão, where a one-hour journey on the back of a lorry cost 1.50. I offered him a 50-*real* note.

'Oh dear, I don't have the right change. Can we make it 40?'

I pulled the note back and rummaged in my pocket. 'Or perhaps we could make it 20,' I said tersely. Suddenly he discovered some one-*real* notes underneath his seat. The *fortalezenses'* ability to coax money from foreigners never failed to impress me.

1142 Assis Street was home to four girls, Nívea, Lívea, Aninha and Rose. All four worked as prostitutes on the Beira-Mar seafront. I had been given the address by Elismar, an officer from the Juvenile Police Unit, and had rung the house that morning asking if I could visit them. Nívea took the call. 'I don't mind, but the others are still asleep,' she said. 'I don't know whether they'd mind.'

I knocked on the door, and Nívea peered out. 'I've spoken to the others and they don't want to speak to you. They said that if you come inside, they'll throw stones at you.'

If I hadn't just paid 34 *reals* for a taxi ride I might have said I would come back another time. 'Oh, I'm sure they'll come round,' I assured her. She reluctantly invited me inside. I sat down on the bare living-room floor and began chatting to Nívea. I could hear the other girls whispering in another room.

'Where do you come from, Nívea?'

'Iguatú. It's a town in the interior, 387 kilometres from here.'

'What brought you to Fortaleza?'

'Well, my dad died from cancer when I was fourteen. My mum was an alcoholic. She drank away all Dad's money.'

'Was he rich?'

'Yeah! He owned a sweet factory.'

As I had suspected, the other girls could not resist joining in the conversation. One by one they came in, still in their dressing gowns, and sat with us on the floor. Before long we were all engaged in an animated discussion.

Lívea was also from Iguatú. She had begun selling her body when she was fifteen – 'after my parents got divorced'. Aninha began on the Beira-Mar seafront when she was fourteen. She had been living on the streets since her father threw her out of the house for getting pregnant. Rose had never known her parents and believed that her aunt and uncle, who had brought her up, did not want her.

'When my parents separated, my whole world fell apart,' Lívea recalled. 'I started selling my body on the town square in Iguatú. I came here to Fortaleza when I was sixteen because I heard that *gringos* pay more – and in dollars.'

'At least you've *got* parents,' interrupted Rose. 'I've only got aunties and uncles. I don't even know what my mum's name was.'

'My mum says she'd rather have had a still-birth than a daughter like me,' Nívea said. 'Believe me, it's better not to know them at all than to know that they hate you ...'

I asked how much money the girls made in a night.

'On a good night, 250 *reals*. Sometimes 1,000 *reals* a week,' said Lívea.

'That's more than the President earns!' I protested.

'Well, we do a better job!' laughed Rose.

Aninha produced a $100 bill. 'That's what I earned last night.'

Lívea was impressed. 'Wow! From that greasy fat Frenchman?'

'You're just jealous,' Aninha taunted.

Every night the girls set off for the promenade. There they waited on street corners between the Iracema and Beira-Mar beaches. They did their deals there before going off in the client's car or a taxi to a motel. Often it was morning by the time they got home, and they would sleep until afternoon.

Nívea said that she preferred foreign tourists. They paid more, and sometimes gave her gifts of perfume and clothes.

'And sometimes Nívea does it for free, 'cos she's a slapper!'

'It's your mother who's the slapper,' Nívea snapped back.

In Brazil, the worst verbal abuse you can commit is to insult somebody's mother. Rose had never known her mother and was visibly upset by Nívea's jibe.

'You're probably right,' she said sulkily, and left the room in tears.

Nívea ignored her departure and carried on talking loudly. 'The Italians are here all year round but you get most in August, the place is full of them. Then in September the Austrians arrive. October is the month the French come. So in three months we have to switch between *"amore"*, *"liebe"* and *"amour"*!'

'And "*soldi*", "*geld*" and "*argent*"!' giggled Lívea.

A few minutes later, a red-faced and swollen-eyed Rose sauntered back into the room.

'You're all making a lot of money,' I said to the foursome. 'What do you plan to do in the future?'

'I want to get rich, buy a big house and drive a flashy car,' said Lívea.

'I want to marry a sailor,' sniffed Rose. 'I want a nice house and lots of children.'

'Not me,' retorted Nívea. 'I don't want to depend on any man. I'm going to be a journalist. Who knows? You might see me reporting on TV one day.'

The others groaned.

'We're all just lost souls, really,' said Aninha conclusively. 'I suppose that's why we get on so well.'

Aninha explained that each of the girls had a nickname. She was the moon, Lívea the sky, Nívea the stars and Rose the sun. 'Rose is called "the flea", too!' she laughed. The others giggled, except Rose, who was much the smallest of the four.

'At least I haven't got stretch marks!' she snapped.

Aninha stopped laughing immediately and glowered at Rose. 'Bitch,' she growled.

I thanked the girls for their time; my over-priced taxi ride had certainly not been a waste

of money. I promised to pass by their 'point'
that evening. I walked for a few blocks on to a
main street, where I caught the bus back to the
beach. The fare was just 80 *centavos*.

I met up later with the girls on the Beira-Mar
seafront. Aninha was standing on the kerbside,
swinging her handbag at passing cars. Lívea
and Nívea were sitting on top of a graffiti-
covered wall. Rose was not there; she had
already been picked up, much to the irritation
of the other girls.

As I stood on the pavement with the girls, a
black jeep pulled up on the opposite side of the
road. The driver shouted 'Fifty *reals*? How
about it?'

I looked at the girls.

'He's talking to *you*,' laughed Aninha. 'That
one prefers men.'

I squirmed in embarrassment and said my
goodbyes hastily. I continued along the promenade at a fast trot, towards the hotels in Beira-Mar.
Turning up a side street I climbed up the hill to the
main road where my bus stopped. On the corner,
besides a Pizza Hut, a young girl wearing Lycra
shorts and a bikini top was sitting on her own on
a brick wall. On the wall somebody had spray-
painted the words *ponto das putas* – 'whores'
point'.

I asked her name.

'Michele.'

You're not from Serviluz, are you?'

'Yeah – why do you ask?'

'Your mum's called Mario do Carmo?'

'How do you know that?'

I explained that I was a friend of Peter and Selma. Her eyes lit up immediately. 'I'm very fond of them. They helped my family, and they've given me a lot of good advice.'

'But did you take the advice?'

Michele's eyes dropped. 'I can't bear to think about my mum. Just to think about her, I start crying. She used to come looking for me, in tears, asking had anyone seen me, showing everyone my photo. I used to hide when I saw her coming. Now she doesn't come looking for me any more.'

'Why don't you go home, then?'

'I do, sometimes – but I never stay there long. I don't know why. My mum even got me a place in the dance class. That's my dream; to be a dancer … a singer, too. But I only went once.'

Michele began working as a prostitute because there was no food at home. She was ten years old at that time.

'The taxi drivers used to pick me up and I'd go with a *gringo*. Then I'd go home and give my mum what I'd earned. She'd ask me where the money came from. I said that I'd stolen it and she used to give me a hiding. But I was too ashamed to tell her how I really got it.'

She told me about the foreign tourists. 'The other day an Italian took me, my friend Tati and

an older girl to a motel, in his car. He put me
and Tati in the boot and the older girl in front so
it wouldn't look like he was taking children in.
He gave me 50 *reals* and a telephone card. He
said I could phone him if I ever needed money
to buy clothes.'

Michele had a rare, heartbreaking realism.
'You know, I used to play with dolls and play-
houses. I never play any more. I'm too young to
be doing this! Look at me – sat here on "whores'
point". I'm not a whore, I'm just a little girl. I
wish I could just turn back the time and go back
to being a child again.'

Tears welled up in my eyes. 'Michele, just go
back home. Your mother wants you back. Peter
and Selma want to help you too. I know that
God will give you a second chance.'

A smile spread across Michele's face. 'Do you
really think so?'

'I'm sure of it.'

'But … Oh, no.'

'What?'

'I haven't got any money for the bus.'

I gave Michele 80 *centavos*. She went to catch
the 466 bus back home.

The next day was my last in Forteleza. I
retuned to Michele's home in Serviluz. Michele
was already back. She showed me a bedroom
she had made for herself in a tiny storage room
underneath the stairs. There was a mattress and
a wooden table, on which she had carefully

arranged her fluffy toys and perfume bottles. Both mother and daughter seemed full of hope. Her mother had already enrolled her at a local dance class.

'I suppose I ought to punish her for running away,' she said apologetically. 'But I can't bring myself to do it. I'm just so happy to have her back.'

9

Belém: The Bat's Hole

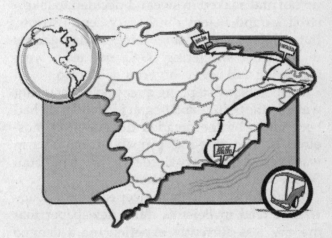

My stomach was churning as I got down from the bus in Belém. I felt as if I was about to vomit, and I was flushed and headachy. The thousand-mile journey from Fortaleza to Belém, in the far north of Brazil on the mouth of the Amazon, had been by bus. The toilet had leaked *again*, and for most of the journey I had been inhaling the stench of sewage. But there was more. My head throbbed, my forehead burned, and my joints ached as if I had walked the whole way.

As I checked into a city-centre hotel I knew that I had come down with a fever. In my room I collapsed onto the bed and turned the air-conditioning fully up. But it did not bring down my high temperature – a few hours later I woke up hot and soaked in sweat. I decided to take a stroll around Belém's busy city centre streets. But while the roadside temperature gauges registered a sweltering 38°C, my teeth were chattering and I was shivering with cold.

I remembered stepping over pools of stagnant water in the Sertão, and began to wonder if I had been bitten by the dreaded dengue-fever mosquito. If I had, it would probably mean my trip was over – a trip that was to have taken me from Belém deep into the Amazon jungle.

I was thrown into even deeper despondency when I read in Belém's daily newspaper that the city was currently experiencing a dengue epidemic. I went back to my room, took a couple of paracetamols and went to bed early. As I lay exhausted, the room spinning wildly around me, I prayed for God's healing. 'Lord, I so want to finish this journey. I know there is so much more you want to show me.' But all my body wanted was to be taken home to England on a stretcher. I dozed off.

I awoke next morning feeling marvellously better. My fever had gone and only a few minor aches and pains were left. Much relieved, I decided to check out the famous *Ver-o-Peso* market on the quayside, just one of the sights for which the city is celebrated. Belém's public spaces and buildings are impressive reminders of its prosperous past: some of its broad streets and avenues lead to the very edge of the forest.

Belém's child prostitution problem is well-documented. Amaury Ribeiro Jr – no relation to Luiz – was a journalist friend from the Brazilian news magazine *Isto É*. I had read his article on child prostitution in the city, in which he described how he had infiltrated some of the inner-city brothels, many of which were owned by French, Portuguese and Italian immigrants and other foreigners. Most of the clients were also foreigners and mostly came from docked cargo ships and oil tankers. One French sailor, Abamar Omar, had told Amaury: 'Belém is the world's sexual paradise. You can get a girl of whatever age you like, whenever you like.'

Amaury's article was entitled 'Foreigners control child prostitution in Belém.' It cited official figures from the city's prosecution service. Of the 114 prostitution points, 77 were exploiting children between the ages of eleven and fourteen. Five of the 77 dealt exclusively in underage girls. Out of the five, four were owned by foreigners.

On my way to the *Ver-o-Peso*, I decided to go down one of the streets Amaury had mentioned. *Primeiro de Março* was a narrow lane running parallel to Belém's main street, and most of the city centre brothels were located there. In contrast to the busy main street, the cobbled lane was almost deserted. A few scantily-clad women stood outside doorways and on street corners. One of them croaked her wheedling invitation to me from across the street.

'Come on love ... you know you want to!'

I did not, I assured her. I hurried on. I had walked for a few blocks when a man came out of one of the houses and walked quickly towards me. I suddenly saw the dull sheen of a revolver barrel poking from his coat towards me. My heart gave a sudden jump. I turned and made a dash for it, down another road that led back to the main street. I managed to lose him by mingling with the crowds of shoppers.

The main street was lined with tall mango trees. A ripe fruit just missed me as it crashed to the ground a few metres away. Some of the parked cars had not been so lucky, as the huge dents in their roofs proved. I was wondering what further dangers lay in store for me, when the heavens opened and I was caught in a sudden equatorial downpour. In a few minutes the roads had become rivers; pedestrians scurried under canopies or into shops, and the city centre traffic was brought to a complete stand-still. I was completely soaked.

As suddenly as it had started, the rain stopped. By the time I arrived at the *Ver-o-Peso* market the sun was blazing again. My clothes were dry and the pools of rain water had already evaporated.

The market spanned the riverfront. My senses were assailed by a profusion of smells, colours and sounds. Hundreds of tiny stalls sold everything from fruit and fish to snake skins and dolphin eyes. In the distance, wooden craft chugged up and down the murky waters of the Amazon, docking at the quay to unload their cargoes.

I wandered round the market for over an hour. The fruit section alone was fascinating, piled with bizarre-looking fruit I had never heard of, let alone seen. The *Piquiá, cajarana* and *saputilha* were round like a tennis ball, with soft fleshy insides. The *pupunha* and *tucumã* were plum-sized berries. The *ingá* was like a pod full of peas, while the *urucurana* was like an egg covered in spiny hooks. There were also some Amazonian fruits that I knew well but were probably just as unfamiliar to first-timers – like the *cupuaçú* and *acerola* with their unique, delicious flavours.

Another part of the market was stacked with natural medicines and strange potions, each labelled with a description of what the user

hoped it would do for them. One was inscribed
'Natural Viagra'; another, *Olho Gordo*, apparently stopped other people being jealous of
you. *Corre Atrás* was a special brew designed to
make a man 'run after' you; *Amansa Mulher*
would have the same effect on women.
Chatting to the stallholder, I speculated on
what would happen if the two were mixed up.
She showed me a powder of cooked lizards
called *Tamaquaré* which women sprinkled over
their husbands to reduce their sexual appetite.
She said it was her most popular product.

'They don't really work, do they?' I chuckled.

'Oh yes they do,' she retorted. 'But only if
you have faith.'

I replaced my 'Irresistible to Women' potion
and moved on.

Alongside the main market was an open-air
canteen. Freshly cooked food was served on
metal-topped counters while huge rats scurried underfoot. Later I discovered that the rat
population of Belém is four million – almost
four times the number of people. Beside barbe-
cued spits and plates of rice, beans and *farinha*
to go, most stalls were selling two regional
dishes. One, *Tacacá*, was a soup made of
prawns with manioc juice, manioc leaves and a
dollop of manioc goo – a slimy green gunk that
reminded me so much of something else that I
could not bring myself to sample it. Instead
I ordered fried fish with liquefied *açaí*, a dark

maroon berry that is mixed with tapioca (another manioc product).

I perched on a stool, dredging my bowl of stodgy *açaí* with a wooden spoon. I felt somebody touch me on the shoulder. It was a barefoot young girl with tangled, dirty hair.

'Will you buy me lunch?'

'Sure,' I replied. I beckoned the stall-holder.

'What about my sister?'

Standing next to her was an older girl, also barefoot.

'All right – sit down.'

'And my friends?'

Soon I was buying food for six ravenous teenagers. They sucked their fried fish methodically to the bone and slurped down their *açaí*, tipping in as much tapioca as they could manage.

'So – where do you all come from?'

'From here,' said one of the boys, his mouth full of food. 'We live on the streets. How about buying us a drink to wash it down?'

'Shut up, Pedro,' said the younger girl indignantly. 'You're so bad-mannered. He's already bought us lunch.'

Her name, it had emerged, was Adrielle. She was thirteen. Her sister Márcia was seventeen.

I bought a two-litre bottle of a fizzy fruit drink. The boys swigged it down straight from the bottle, belched loudly, and then ran off between the market stalls.

I asked Adrielle and Márcia about their family.

'My dad was stabbed to death in a bar fight,' said Márcia. 'Mum started living with another man who beat us up all the time. He'd leave my little sister black and blue. I told her she had to choose between him and us.'

'And she chose him,' added Adrielle calmly.

'We started living on the streets,' continued Márcia. 'That was two years ago.'

'How do you make money?'

'The boys steal things or look after stalls at night. And the girls …' Adrielle paused. 'Well, we sell *ourselves*, don't we? What else have we got to sell?'

She spent her day in the market, she told me. 'I sell my body to the stall-holders, or to men from the boats in the harbour. I use the money to buy clothes, shampoo, face cream, that sort of stuff.'

'You don't do it without a condom, right?'

Adrielle's brow furrowed. 'A what?'

I was shocked. 'Adrielle, do you know what AIDS is?'

'Oh yes – it's a disease.'

'Right. And how do you catch it?'

Adrielle thought hard. 'From drinking dirty water?'

Little Adrielle should not have needed to know what a condom was. And for most thirteen-year-olds, mixing up AIDS and cholera would not have been such a catastrophic mistake.

'Where do you spend the night?'

'In the Bat's Hole. It's a sewer under the market. It's our den. We sleep there and that's where we go when we need to hide from the police. Want to see it?'

I followed Adrielle to the edge of the quay. There was a metal manhole cover in the ground. The thiteen-year-old lifted it with practised ease. Underneath was a cavity, flooded by river water. Adrielle jumped down feet-first, landing expertly on a concrete ledge a few metres below. From there she hopped on to a wooden post. Trying to do the same, I missed the ledge completely and ended up knee-deep in water. Adrielle giggled. 'It's OK. You have to wade the rest, anyway.'

She led me through the murky water towards a huge round tunnel some six metres across. Adrielle pulled herself up and I followed her, peering through the gloom.

What appeared to be a large group of young boys and girls was gathered, standing or crouching in the dark tunnel. Some were sniffing from bags of glue. Down the centre of the pipe, a stream of sewage trickled into the water in which I was standing. I choked as my lungs tried to get used to the stale foul smell that was everywhere.

'Who's he?' somebody demanded. 'What's he doing here?' A black teenager emerged from the tunnel brandishing a dangerous-looking flick-knife.

'Leave him alone, he's a good guy.' My defender was Pedro, whom I had treated to lunch earlier. His friend snapped his knife shut and stepped reluctantly back, still eyeing me mistrustfully. Pedro showed me a silver watch he had just snatched from an unfortunate shopper.

The Bat's Hole was like a Victorian thieves' kitchen, a set-piece from one of Fagin's scenes in *Oliver Twist*. The pitiful state of these youngsters, huddled in secrecy beside a running stream of sewage, had a kind of inverted glamour because of the dramatic gloom and the small pools of light that found their way through gaps in the pipe and painted the faces of the children with a dull silvery light. I dreaded to think what germs hung in that fetid air, or how many cases of juvenile pneumonia, malaria and other diseases these boys and girls contracted.

'Couldn't you have found a better place than a sewer?' I asked Adrielle.

'It's the only place that's safe,' she explained. 'The police don't dare to come down here to beat us up.'

The kids in the Bat's Hole made me stay until every one of them had written his or her name in my notebook. They made me promise to come back with comics and colouring books.

I made my way back through the manhole, hauled myself back to the surface, and walked back up Belém's main street, my clothes dripping, to my hotel. I tiptoed past Reception, but it was impossible to disguise the fact that I and my clothes stank of sewage.

In my room, I took a very long shower. It seemed to take for ever to get rid of the smell – for days afterwards I thought I caught occasional whiffs of it. After my shower I rubbed myself down and put on some clean clothes.

My next appointment was with Marcel Hazeu, a researcher with the Emaús Movement in Belém. The movement had recently carried out a study of prostitution in remote regions of the Amazon. Marcel was someone I had been anxious to meet, and I had arranged to do so even before I arrived in Belém. I wanted to ask his advice about the next leg of my journey.

'So little is being said about the plight of children in the Amazon,' he said as he shook my hand.

Belém has always been a gateway to the Amazon forests. The city was founded by the Portuguese in 1615, and was the first European colony along the Amazon. The river and its opening up accounts for Belém's commercial importance: since the nineteenth century it has been a centre for foreign traders.

Prostitution, explained Marcel, came to the Amazon along with the discovery of gold. The ancient jungle, once virtually impenetrable once you left the broad waters of the great river, had recently been opened up by ambitious road-building programmes. The might of the Amazon had been harnessed in huge dam projects – the river has the greatest volume of water of all the world's rivers.

Slowly one of the few remaining unknown regions of the world had been penetrated and slowly destroyed; every month, tracts of the forest were falling to the chainsaws as the demands of softwood exporters and beef farmers took precedence over the much less visible resources of the forest.

'The government offered incentives to foreign development companies and sponsored large-scale mining projects for bauxite, iron and other minerals. The whole area became a magnet for migration. The population grew from a few million to over thirteen million today, and the growth rate in the Amazon is more than twice the national average.'

Most of the new arrivals were men, drawn by the chance to *bamburrar* – to get rich quick. Preservation of the environment and respect for the life and culture of other people meant very little to them. 'They brought with them diseases that wiped out whole tribes of Indians. And they brought another white man's disease, too – prostitution.'

Marcel's researchers spent many months visiting remote mining towns deep in the jungle.

They had uncovered an organised network of prostitution involving girls as young as twelve and thirteen years old. The girls were recruited in the larger towns and cities and sent to work as prostitutes in the mining towns. 'They're promised jobs as cleaners or cooks, but when they get to the mining town they're forced to work in the brothels. They are told that until they've paid off the cost of their plane ticket they aren't allowed to leave.'

Marcel suggested that I should go first to Santarém, a town on the Amazon five hundred miles inland from Belém, and near to the Tapajós River basin where most of the gold mines were located. It was one of the main places where girls were recruited and trafficked. He pre- sented me with a copy of his finished report and details of some contacts in Santarém.

I stood up to leave. Marcel shook my hand and held it momentarily. 'Be very careful. The gold mines are lawless places. They are run by *pistoleiros* – hired gunmen. Once they suspect you're an impostor, you won't get out alive.'

The quayside was piled high with bags of rice, long metal girders and a tractor motor, all destined for Santarém. I arrived just ten minutes before the boat was due to leave, and they had still not finished loading. I clutched my luggage and stepped carefully up the wobbly gangplank. I had reserved a hammock-hook on the second floor: I located the staircase and went to look for my hook.

The boat was already packed with people, and the deck was criss-crossed by hammocks, with piles of bags and boxes alongside. I decided I had an excellent case for suing the boat company for what the Brazilians call *propaganda enganosa* – misleading advertising. 'Reserved' was a word misleading in the extreme. The crew assured me there was a spare hammock-hook somewhere, I just needed to find it. Later I discovered that seasoned travellers on the Amazon turn up the day before their boat is due to leave, so that they can secure a good space.

I finally found the last remaining hook, between an overweight chain-smoker and a grizzled old woman with no teeth. I hung up my hammock, but there was no space to lie down. Instead I leaned over the side and watched the rest of the cargo being loaded.

By the time the last box had been thrown aboard, the boat was three hours late in leaving. As well as the endless sacks of rice, oranges, *farinha* and crates of *Cerpa* beer, there were also stacks of televisions, stereo systems and a few fridge freezers, all of which had to be found space and made secure. Space was even found for two motorcycles and a pick-up truck. It was nearly nightfall by the time the boat finally chugged sluggishly out of port and the lights of Belém faded into the distance.

We journeyed up the Amazon for three days and three nights. I hardly slept at all. I soon discovered that it is impossible to lie on your front in a hammock. It is not a good idea to move on a crowded hammock deck, for the slightest movement sets all the other hammocks rocking like a Newton's Cradle. The most difficult part was getting into the hammock in the first place. Getting one leg in was easy, but I never managed to swing the rest of myself into place without elbowing somebody in the face, getting somebody else's foot in my mouth or spinning round too far and ending up with my face on the floor – or in somebody else's face. A few times during the night the toothless old woman slapped me on the backside, peered over my hammock with a gummy grin and said, 'Sorry – did I disturb you?' I smiled nervously back and told her I had not felt a thing.

In the end I decided it would be better to stay awake, and in the morning fell out of my hammock with an aching neck and hunched back, wondering why on earth I had not spent the extra 20 *reals* and booked a cabin.

During the trip I also became as familiar as I wished to be with *brega*, north Brazil's most popular type of music. It blasted out from the boat's loudspeakers all day and most of the night. *Brega* means 'tacky' in Portuguese, which sums up the music perfectly. It is a kind of 1960s slow rock, with lyrics such as 'If you chakataka with me, I'll chakataka with you' and 'I won't sleep with you (unless you use a condom)'. Every evening there was a live *brega* performance in the bar at the top of the boat, with live cover versions of popular hits.

But the inconveniences paled beside the sheer loveliness of this, the second-longest river in the world. The silt-laden Amazon was at times so wide that one could barely see the other side. In these waters can be found exotic plants such as the world's largest water lilies, with vast green pads that are so big that they can actually cause environmental damage to the waters in which they flourish. The forest itself was layered with millions of shades of green, and alive with droning insects and chirping parakeets. Pink fresh-water dolphins played in the boat's wash as we chugged majestically along.

This was the mighty Amazon River in all its splendour. I could hardly believe I was here.

10

Santarém: Engraved on the palm of my hands

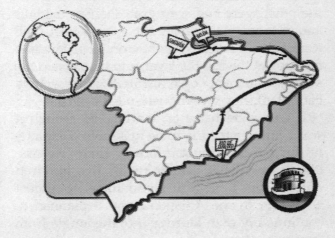

Ahead, a long way downriver, I could see fireflies swarming in the jungle haze. I peered into the night, watching the specks of light juddering up and down, making small circles in the gloom. As the boat made its slow progress the lights became bigger and brighter, until I realised that they were not fireflies at all, but the lights of Santarém. We had been on the river for three days and three nights.

As we approached the town, the pilot cut back the engines. The boat settled into a new, slower chug-chugging as we made a wide turn across the river to the docks. It was 4.30 am. A pall of smoke from the engine room billowed up as the craft, with much grumbling and creaking of timbers, came to a halt, swaying against the dockside as ropes were thrown and secured and the passengers began to grab their belongings and position themselves for a quick exit onto terra firma. I lingered awhile on deck, taking a last look at the mighty river, and then joined the other stream, of people negotiating the wobbly gangplank and precariously-piled cargo.

It was good to be on land again, though it was a strange feeling to be in a town completely surrounded by rainforest. There was no bigger town than Santarém for five hundred miles. From here, you could travel to almost anywhere in the Amazon basin. I planned to continue my own journey into the jungle from Santarém.

When I explored the town later that morning it did not feel so isolated. The town centre was busy and crowded, and the quayside was lined with hundreds of brightly-painted wooden boats, most of them named after their owner or his wife. Some were named after St

Bartholemew, the patron saint of the river, or Yara, the water princess. One fishing boat was called 'Jesus Gave Me This' – obviously owned by a grateful believer. Alongside the boats on the jetty, their loads were spread out: huge watermelons, clusters of bananas, jute, buckets of ripe *açaí* berries, brazil nuts in rock-hard shells and many types of fish.

There were many varieties of river craft. The 'water buses' were twin-decked passenger boats, each of which carried a sign with its destination and departure time. Some of the destinations had enchanting Indian names, like Itacoatiara, Itaituba, Juruna, Maués and Oriximiná. In the Indian language, *tupí-guraní*, the names were even more intriguing: Painted Stone, Gravelly Place, Black Mouths, Chattering Parrots, Angry Bees.

The local people called the Amazon *estrada liquida*, the watery highway. Santarém's roads were primitive – unmetalled, and waterlogged for most of the year, and the river was the town's only lifeline. As well as the water buses, there were water taxis, a floating police station, and even a floating Esso petrol station; it looked exactly like a normal one, except that it bobbed up and down with the waves. It even had a 'Hungry Tiger' shop.

I left the waterfront behind and climbed the hill beside the white Baroque church that stood, like so many other white Baroque churches I had seen, in the town square. After several blocks I arrived at a day centre run by the Catholic Pastoral Service. In Belém, Marcel had suggested I should visit the centre, which offered assistance of all kinds to needy children and their families.

I introduced myself to Bernadette, who was in charge of the centre's work with girls. She showed me round. 'The centre gives help to more than three hundred needy children every day, and also gives help and advice to their parents.'

I asked Bernadette if what Marcel had told me was right – that Santarém is a focal point for trafficking in young girls in the Amazon region.

Bernadette nodded. 'Organised gangs in the town recruit young girls and send them to the mining towns. Sometimes the gangs wait at the school gates and entice them from there ... there's a lot of money to be made.' She had lost count, she said, of the number of families that had come to the centre and pleaded with her to find their missing daughters. Most of the girls were never seen again. A few who had managed to escape had horrific stories to tell, of how they had been kept as slaves in brothels, deep in the jungle.

'Once we rescued a thirteen-year-old girl. She was called Lúcia. She told us that she had tried to escape once, but the brothel-keeper

had gone after her and recaptured her. He tied
her to the back of his car and dragged her along
the road, back to the brothel. When they were
back, he rubbed raw lemon juice into her open
wounds.'

A group of boys was playing a noisy five-a-side
soccer match on a concrete football pitch, shouting and screaming as the game became more
and more hectic. I was wondering how I could
get to a gold mine to interview the girls for
myself. Bernadette seemed to be aware of what
I was thinking.

'Of course, you don't have to leave Santarém to
find girls who have been forced into prostitution.'

'No?'

'Oh no. You can find them right here. Follow
me.'

At the far side of the football pitch, a young
girl with Indian features was sitting on a bench,
cradling a tiny bundle in her arms.

'This is Fabíola. She is fourteen. Her baby has
only just been born.'

The baby had clear skin and bright blue eyes.

'What is her name?'

'Yasmin,' replied Fabíola. She clutched her
baby to her defensively. 'My mum wants me to
give her away.'

'Why?'

'She says, it's bad enough having me, without having my baby as well,' she whispered.

I persuaded Fabíola to tell me her story. She had been conceived in a brothel in a gold mine where her mother had been working as a prostitute. Her mother resented her, because her father had been a white man.

'She said she should have killed me while I was still in her tummy,' said Fabíola, her voice barely audible. 'One day she went to the *pai de santo* and put a curse on me. She made a wish, that I would die under the wheels of a car.'

Once she was 11, Fabíola had been sent to the docks with instructions to sell herself to the boat people. 'If you don't come home with at least 50 *reals*, I'll give you a thrashing.'

'And how much did you charge?' I asked.

'Four *reals*. My mum said I was only worth that.'

I was appalled. 'But that's – how many times a night?'

'Fifteen.'

Even shocked as I was, I could have done the mathematics. I wanted to hear it from her own lips.

It seemed that every twist and turn my journey took, fresh depths of evil were opening up. To hear of a mother quite so unfeeling was perhaps not so unusual. But there was something indescribably chilling in this fourteen-year-old's account of her initiation into the same sordid life that her mother had led. The bare numbers, uttered in a calm, matter-of-fact way, told their own horrific story as my mind manipulated them. Assume that she started work at six and finished, say, at eight next morning, before wearily dragging herself home and crashing into whatever space she slept in. That made fourteen hours. In other words, every hour, more or less, all through the night, every night, this child had sex with men. And she had started doing so when she was just eleven years old.

'I came home once and I had earned 49 *reals* and 50 *centavos*. My mum took the money and threw it back into my face. It wasn't enough, she said. She thrashed me with a *cueira* vine and sent me back to the docks.' The *cueira* is a climbing tree, covered in spiny thorns. 'After that I never came back without 50 *reals*. Sometimes I stayed on the streets for two or three days without eating or sleeping until I'd made enough money. I was terrified of going home without the right amount.'

I looked at the baby. 'Who is Yasmin's father?'

'Oh, he was just a man ... he raped me. Then he threatened to shoot me in the head if I told anybody. But that doesn't matter. I'm going to bring up my daughter well. Do you know, I thought that when she was born I would resent her. But when I saw her I couldn't help it, I began to love her. Now I wouldn't give her up, not for anything.'

She paused, then looked up at me. 'Why couldn't my mum love me like that?'

When night falls in the Amazon, the heavens explode in colour. The sky turns fiery red, then deep purple-dappled indigo, slowly changing to a dark blue streaked with amber and scarlet. Finally all the colours run together like a rain-soaked watercolour. As the sun sets, the sky is perforated by thousands of bright stars.

I was walking under such a sky, along a dimly-lit road near the centre of Santarém. I was going to the house of Rita, mother of a group of girls whom Bernadette knew. A single street lamp flickered on and off, off and on, surrounded by a haze of insects. As I approached the house I could see the bulky silhouette of a very obese woman in a rocking chair on a dark patio. A cigarette glowed between her fingers.

I walked up the dirt driveway and began to introduce myself. She cut me short.

'What do you want?'

'*Dona* Rita?'

'Who wants to know?' She took a long drag on her cigarette. Smoke poured from her mouth and nose. Even in the dim patio light she was a disgusting sight, slumped in the rocking chair, mounds of flesh shifting as she rocked back and forth. I offered her my hand cautiously.

'My name's Matt. I'm from England. I'd like to talk to you about your daughters.'

She ignored my hand and glared at me. 'My daughters are all shameless whores. How's that?' Her voice, ravaged by too many cigarettes, was a gruff bark. I laughed nervously.

'*Dona* Rita, I'd like to ask you a few questions.'

'So what are you waiting for?'

The interview was obviously to be out of doors; she seemed permanently wedged into the rocking chair. I pulled up a three-legged chair and perched on it. Looking up into Rita's unlovely face I could see straight up her ragged nostrils. She had several warts in her face and the beginnings of a wiry beard.

I had only one question, but I came at it obliquely.

'How many daughters do you have, *Senhora*?'

'Six. The oldest is Soraia – she's thirty-one now. Then Paula – I don't know her age. Cândida's nineteen and Ana Cláudia sixteen. Ana Cláudia's the most troublesome, but then she's not really mine; I adopted her when she was a baby. But the only two that live with me are Jéssica and Marciane. They're thirteen and eleven.'

'Where are the others?'

'You want the honest truth?

I nodded.

'I don't know. I don't care. I'm glad to be rid of them, to tell you the truth. They're all *vagabundas*, those girls. All of them. They've got no shame at all. I don't know what I did wrong,

I really don't. I brought them all up well, like I'm bringing up my youngest two. Wanna see them?'

She did not wait for my reply but bawled into the house behind her. Two young girls promptly appeared and stood timidly at their mother's side.

'It's all Ana Cláudia's fault. I don't know why I took pity on her. Her own mother didn't want her. That whore started *giving* herself to men when she was eight! And because of her Cândida started selling herself, you know. Ana Cláudia once sold her for a lollipop. And the others – they're all *perdidas* – lost causes – I've washed my hands of all of them.'

But Rita was not telling me the whole truth. Her daughters were certainly prostitutes; Bernadette had told me that already. And it was true that most of them had run away from home. But they had fled from a mother who had been prepared to sell her own daughters as prostitutes. She had even had three bedrooms built on to the back of the house. In these rooms, she forced her daughters to attend to her customers.

I was sickened by the woman's hypocritical ranting and raging. I decided to confront her with what I knew.

'Didn't you used to sell your own daughters, *Senhora*? Isn't that why they're *perdidas*, eh? Wasn't it you who used to make them *give* themselves to men for money?'

Rita lurched forward, the runners of her chair creaking under her vast weight, and looked as if she were about to swallow me up whole.

'If I hadn't sold them, the whores would have done it for free,' she spluttered, spraying me with spittle.

'What kind of mother sells her own daughters?' I persisted.

'How *dare* you!' she bellowed, her double chin wobbling. 'Get out, you hear? Get out! Get out!'

Next morning I met up with Bernadette outside the day centre. She knew where Ana Cláudia, Rita's adopted daughter, was hiding. I was keen to hear Ana Cláudia's side of the story.

As we walked down the road away from the day centre we came across Fabíola in a bus shelter. She was holding her baby limply in her arms and was trembling and whimpering. Baby clothes and nappies were strewn over the pavement beside her. When she saw us, she burst into tears.

'Whatever's the matter?' I asked.

'I went to the day centre but it was all locked up ... and I haven't get any money to get back home.'

Bernadette stroked her hair gently. 'Shhh ... it's because it's Carnival Day. Everything closes today.'

Fabíola's sobs stopped and she wiped her eyes. She had been awake all night with a fever, she said, but her mother had refused to help her. 'So in the morning I packed some baby things ...' – she indicated the nappies and clothes forlornly – 'and got the bus to the day centre. Then I found it was closed. I didn't know what to do.' She sniffed miserably and wiped her nose with her sleeve.

She certainly looked unwell. I put my hand to her forehead; it was burning. 'She's running a temperature,' I said to Bernadette.

'We should take her to the hospital,' she decided. 'There'll be a doctor on duty there.'

On the way to the hospital we stopped at a chemist, where Fabíola took a paracetamol.

Before we saw the doctor, Fabíola had her temperature taken. It had fallen; the paracetamol had done its job.

'I'm afraid the doctor won't be able to see her,' said the receptionist severely, peering at us through a window in her office. 'She hasn't got a temperature.'

'But she's just taken a paracetamol. That was why we gave it her – she was running a high temperature, she was really ill.'

'Well, she hasn't got a temperature now,' the receptionist said sharply. 'And if she hasn't got a temperature, the doctor won't see her. I'm sorry.' She slid the shutter across the window, and that was that.

Fabíola was already asleep on a bench in the waiting room. Baffled by the way the system worked, we went back to the chemist and bought some more tablets. We gave them to Fabíola along with her bus fare home.

We waited at the bus-stop as she clutched her baby and the bag of clothes and nappies. The bus came and Fabíola and her baby climbed on board. As it pulled away, she burst into tears again.

I had never seen a tarantula on its hind legs – in fact, I had never seen a tarantula. The *caranjeira* tarantula was about the size of my foot, its body alone the size of my fist. As I got closer, it wriggled six hairy limbs in the air, gnawing its poison-tipped fangs and hissing malevolently. I prodded it with a stick. The angry arachnid suddenly leapt up at me. I stepped sideways and it missed me by inches. Undeterred, it unleashed its secret weapon: I was sprayed with hundreds of itchy hairs. I ran off down the road, frantically scratching my arms and legs. As I ran, I looked back. The triumphant tarantula was shaking its hairy legs at me, as if to say, 'Come back and fight, you coward!' Then a lorry loaded with gas cylinders came up behind it and squashed it.

Bernadette and I were walking down an uneven earth road on the outskirts of Santarém. Besides the ferocious spiders, green lizards and huge iguanas darted out of the undergrowth as we passed. I could hear then rustling in the grass, but they still scared me half to death when they suddenly jumped out in front of me, flickering their forked tongues and wiggling their bodies from side to side.

The road eventually led to a clearing, in which was a row of crudely-constructed wooden houses, each surrounded by a wattle fence.

Ana Cláudia was staying at her friend's house. She was small and stubby, a *mestiça* with Indian features. Only sixteen years old, she looked much older. Her eyes had a deep, painful expression. She spoke slowly and deliberately.

I asked her why she was hiding from her mother.

'Mum always hated me because I wasn't her real daughter. She brought me up with kicks and punches. I couldn't take it any more. Look ...'

She showed me a deep scar on her side. Down her arms were circular burn marks, made by cigarette stubs. 'She used to hit me around the head with a frying pan. Then she'd rub my face in the dirt on the ground. Once she tried to stab me with a kitchen knife.'

As soon as Ana Cláudia reached the age of ten, her mother started selling her and her sisters, twelve-year-old Cândida and eleven-year-old Nazaré. I hadn't heard about Nazaré. 'Where does she live?' I asked.

'Nazaré got AIDS. She died ... The men were mostly really old. They were around sixty or seventy. They came to our house and Mum made us do it in our bedrooms with them. She set the price and took the money – usually 10 *reals*. She never gave us more than 50 *centavos*. There was a bar on the street in front of our house where my mum sold *cachaça* rum. She got the men drunk then sent them over to us. She made us wait for them in our bedrooms.'

Ana Cláudia dreaded her monthly menstruation. It meant she could not work for her mother. 'She punished us for having our periods. She used to put a spoon on the fire and when it got hot she put it into our mouths and burnt our tongues.'

Rita was without doubt a vicious sadist as well as a brutal exploiter of her own children's innocence. There seemed little I could say to comfort Ana Cláudia. Her scars were not the kind that healed in a few weeks or years. Many carry such scars for a lifetime.

On an impulse, I asked her if she had a Bible in the house. She produced one; many Brazilian homes have a Bible, though in many it is not often read. I turned to the book of Isaiah.

'I'm going to read you something, Ana Cláudia. This is a promise from God.' Tears welled up in her eyes as I read from the forty-ninth chapter of Isaiah.

Can a mother forget the baby at her breast and
have no compassion on the child she has borne?
Though she may forget, I will not forget you! See,
I have engraved you on the palms of my hands.

I closed the book. Tears were rolling down Ana
Cláudia's cheeks. I was choking back tears
myself. I had often read that passage to the
street girls in Belo Horizonte, many of whom
had been abandoned by their mothers. But this
time, in that forest clearing with a young girl
whose existence had been marked by so much
rejection and suffering, those words had fresh
meaning: God loved her, more than anybody
could love her. More than the most devoted
mother. And he would never forget her – he
had written her name on the palms of his
hands.

'Promise me something,' said Ana Cláudia.
'What?'
'Write down everything I told you. Don't
leave anything out. I want people to know my
story.'
As the bus bumped along the road back to
the town centre I was still thinking about Ana
Cláudia's dreadful story.
I'll keep my promise, I vowed. People needed
to know that deep in the Amazon rainforest
something more precious even than plants and
animals is being destroyed. All over the world

powerful voices are raised in protest over the wholesale destruction of the forest. Yet in the same region young girls are being stripped of their rights and their dignity, being robbed of the chance to have a childhood. And nobody seemed to be raising their voices over that at all.

Over the next few days Fabíola's health grew worse. In the end she was rushed into intensive care and put on a drip. She was diagnosed with dengue fever, hepatitis, bronchitis and tuberculosis, all caused by spending too many nights on the streets. Her baby, too, had come down with a fever. The hospital doctor said they should have been admitted days ago.

On my last day in Santarém I went to the hospital with Bernadette to see Fabíola. She had been moved with her baby to the maternity ward, where male visitors were not allowed. I paced up and down in the waiting room like an expectant father, while Bernadette went through to the ward.

After half an hour Bernadette had still not emerged. I decided to break the rules. I sneaked past the receptionist, dodged a few doctors and eventually found the ward. Bernadette was sitting at Fabíola's bedside.

'If the matron finds you here she'll kill you!' hissed Bernadette.

'I just wanted to say goodbye,' I explained.

Fabíola was lying on her back on clean sheets, a soft pillow under her head and a blanket drawn up to her chin. I wondered whether she had ever slept before in a clean, pleasant bed. A bag of fluid hung over the bed and a tube ran down to a needle in her arm. Baby Yasmin lay in a cot by her side, sleeping peacefully. Fabíola looked up at me and smiled. She seized my hand and clasped it tightly.

'You won't forget me, will you?'

Tears blurred my eyes. 'Of course I won't,' I said gruffly.

'Promise?'

'Promise.'

11

Oriximiná: Hell in Paradise Ville

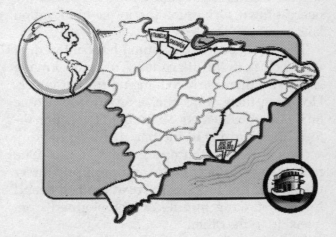

I was determined to visit a mining town. Over the next few days I made a number of enquiries without success. The nearest gold mine was 150 miles deep into the jungle. You could only get there by private plane, or a four-day journey by boat followed by a fifteen-hour hike.

The flight cost 250 *reals*, well outside my budget.

I finally found a mine that could be reached by boat. Even so, it was two hundred miles away. It was a bauxite mine, hidden in the dense jungles along the Trombetas River near the border with Guyana and Surinam. A friend of Bernadette had a brother–in–law who worked there; his name was Cézar, and he said he would meet me there and give me a place to stay. It would mean first taking a boat to the nearest town, Oriximiná (or, in the local Indian language, 'Angry Bees').

The water bus to Oriximiná left Santarém at four o'clock in the afternoon. This time, I made sure I was there early to hang up my hammock. However, there were only a few dozen people on board, mostly men. They spent the entire fifteen-hour journey in the bar, drinking rowdily accompanied by thumping *brega* music. One man smashed a beer bottle and promptly threw up all over the deck. As the boat lurched to and fro, the stinking puddle of sick slopped from one side to the other.

In the middle of the night we sailed into a swarm of black beetles. They were attracted by the boat's lights and flew at them suicidally, dropping in their thousands onto the deck. I stayed wrapped up in my hammock, but even then some of the beetles managed to fall on my clothes and down the back of my neck. When the sun came up, the insects were all dead on their backs, or drowned in vomit.

There were two teenagers on the boat. They shared a hammock, and were being accompanied by a man with long hair tied in a pigtail. That morning I was standing near one of the girls; we were both leaning over the boat's wooden railings. She called across to me.

'Do you know what time we arrive?'

I shook my head. 'I've never been before.'

'Me neither.'

She was called Cleneide, and was fifteen years old. Her friend Cláudia was sixteen. Cleneide told me that they were both from Santarém.

'Are you going to the mining town?' I asked.

'No – we're going to *Vila Paraíso.*' I had not heard of the place, whose name meant 'Paradise Ville'. I asked her where it was.

'Dunno,' she replied. '*He*'s taking us.' She pointed to the long-haired man, who was standing by the girls' hammock. 'He's got us a job as barmaids there.'

'Who is he?'

'The owner of the bar, or something.'

Cleneide went off to join the others for breakfast.

Later that morning, as the boat was arriving at Oriximiná, Cleneide approached me.

'Uh – what I said earlier. Forget it. Actually I'm going to visit my uncle.'

'What?'

'My uncle. He works at the mine. I'm going to visit him.'

'But you said ...'

'I know, but ... I forgot. I'm visiting my uncle. *Really*,' she repeated imploringly.

She was glancing nervously at the long-haired man, who stared coldly back at her.

At Oriximiná, Cézar was waiting for me at the jetty. We took a smaller passenger boat for the next leg of the journey; it would take another three hours to get to Porto Trombetas, the mining town. As the boat ploughed noisily through the smooth black waters of the Trombetas River, Cézar told me about the bauxite mine.

'Around five thousand men work there. Most at the quarry face, deep in the jungle. A twelve-mile-long conveyor belt carries the rocks from the quarry to the plant, to be processed.'

Twelve million tonnes of bauxite were mined every year, he told me. Since mining began around twenty years ago, over one hundred million tonnes had been extracted. There was enough left to keep the mine going for another eighty years.

'Most of it's exported. Freighters come here from all over the world.'

Cézar told me that his sister-in-law had told him why I was in Porto Trombetas. I asked him about prostitution in the town.

'There's a place called *Vila Paraíso* where all the brothels are. It's also called Forty-Five, because it takes a forty-five minute motorboat journey to get there.'

So that was where Cleneide and her friend were heading. 'It's a few miles downstream from the town, on the river bank. There's nothing there except brothels.'

Cézar lived with his wife and four-year-old daughter in one of a row of tiny houses in Porto Trombetas. His wife was preparing lunch when we arrived. Neither of them had ever met me before, yet I was welcomed as if I were family. It is one of the most endearing qualities of Brazilians. In another act of goodwill, one of his friends agreed to lend us his speedboat to make the journey to *Vila Paraíso* later that afternoon.

The 'speedboat' turned out to be a flimsy fibreglass launch about the size of a bathtub, with a rusting outboard motor. I pushed it out from its moorings while Cézar connected the fuel pipe to the drum of diesel that we had filled on the way down. He pulled the cord until the motor grudgingly spluttered into life, vibrating violently in an ugly clatter.

The Trombetas was a smooth corridor of black water, gently ebbing and flowing between thick walls of green; the overhanging branches were entwined with creepers. Its bow tilted upwards, the launch ploughed a watery furrow through the placid river. We kept close to the banks, for the wash from one of the huge ocean-going freighters could easily have capsized a small craft like ours. At the tiller, Cézar told me one of those stories one would prefer not to hear while sitting in a bath-tub in an Amazonian river.

'The other night, I came fishing near here,' he shouted over the din of the outboard motor. 'I was just going to leave when this enormous crocodile came out of the water. Its mouth was huge – and wide open! The brute was about ten feet long!'

I gulped and egged the boat on. Half an hour later we came to a clearing in the forest. There were about twenty rickety wooden shacks, balanced on stilts at the water's edge. It looked like one of the riverbank *favelas* I had seen in Recife. A wooden landing stage jutted out into the river where another small boat was moored.

'*Vila Paraíso!*' shouted Cézar, and cut the motor back a notch. We chugged slowly towards the shore.

As we approached I could make out the wooden structures more clearly. Some were edged with flashing red lights. Outside each was painted the brothel's name: 'Come Closer', 'Moon Shadow', 'It Shakes But It Doesn't Fall' – the last probably a reference to the shaky stilts. One was painted bright pink and called 'Paradise Drinks'. The familiar *brega* music drifted across the calm waters to us.

A number of people were standing outside the bars. As we came up to the jetty, I recognised the long-haired man from the boat. Cleneide and Cláudia were with him. He was leaning against the wooden rails of Paradise Drinks, swigging a bottle of beer. He turned as the boat approached, saw me, and quickly ushered the girls away.

I jumped from the boat and hurried along the wooden jetty, climbing the pink steps of 'Paradise Drinks'. When I got to the top the man and girls were nowhere to be seen.

The bamboo floor was scattered with tables and chairs. At one of the tables two girls were sitting. They were wearing low-cut dresses and red lipstick. They were painting each other's nails.

'Where did that man go?' I panted.

'A *man*?'

'Yeah – a man ... well, a *bicha* ... with long hair. He was standing over there with two girls ...'

'We're the only girls here,' said one of them. '*I* haven't seen a man. Have you seen a man, Tati?'

'Me? Oh, no.' And both girls exploded in giggles.

Cézar and I decided to look round some of the other brothels before returning to Paradise Drinks. I was worried that I might have blown my cover when I talked to the girl on the boat; everybody seemed to be suspicious of us.

I talked with two girls in 'Dona Maria's Bar', a rotting shack perched over the river mud flats. Joice was eighteen years old, and Cristiane was twenty. Joice asked me to buy her a token for the jukebox. She went over, chose a song and sat down again. I asked the girls how they came to be at Dona Maria's.

'Well, I got pregnant. My parents gave me so much grief, I just left. I ended up here.'

Another girl arrived at our table. She lounged back on the plastic chair and stretched her legs out, resting them on Cristiane's knees.

'Are you a *federal*?' she asked, without pre-amble.

'A what?'

'A *federal* – a policeman. Everyone's saying that you're the police.'

I laughed nervously. 'I'm English. I couldn't be a policeman even if I wanted to.'

'So why are you asking so many questions?'

It was dark outside and the atmosphere in the bar was tense. I was suddenly aware that we were in the middle of the jungle, in a lawless region controlled by gangsters and *pistoleiros* – and we were being accused of being under-cover policemen. We decided to leave while we still could.

First, though, I wanted to go to Paradise Drinks again.

The bar was now packed with drinking men and flirting women. The music was turned full up and pounding *brega* music shook the floor. Beneath the slowly revolving multi-dots of a disco mirror lamp, they drank and danced boisterously, shaking the wooden structure.

The girls were chatting to the men. Occasionally a girl would get up and lead a man through a doorway at the far side of the bar. I decided to see where they were going. The doorway led into a maze of dark corridors, with walls and floor of bamboo and doors that clearly led to bedrooms where girls entertained their clients. I followed one narrow passage until I reached the back of the building. A young blonde girl was sitting on a wooden plank, her legs dangling. She looked round, startled.

'Who are you?'

'It's all right,' I replied. 'My name's Matt. I'm from England.'

She turned round to face me. She seemed distraught. '*Senhor*, you've got to get me out of here.'

She was a fifteen-year-old from Santarém. Her name was Bambaloo. She had come to *Vila Paraíso* thinking that she was going to work as a maid in a family house. The brothel owner Santana had offered her the job. But when she arrived at Oriximiná, she had been put on a boat and brought to the brothel.

'He says I can't leave until I've paid off my debts,' she told me. 'But the debt keeps getting bigger – he charges me for the rent of the room, even for the food I eat. And if I don't sleep with someone, he charges me a five-*real* fine.' She was sobbing now. 'Please, *Senhor*, don't forget about me.'

I promised Bambaloo I would do what I could, and hurried back to the bar, conscious of people watching me curiously as I emerged from the doorway. Cézar was waiting for me anxiously. I was aware of hostile eyes following us as we walked down the steep wooden steps back to the jetty. We untied the launch, jumped in and cast off.

Cézar pulled the ignition cord. It spluttered and immediately died. He tried again; it whirred lifelessly. As the boat drifted further and further from the bank he pulled again and again. Finally he picked up the fuel drum. It was completely empty. 'We've been sabotaged! Someone's emptied out all the diesel!'

The boat had drifted into a strong current and was now being dragged out of control downstream. Soon the lights of *Vila Paraíso* had disappeared, and even the faint sound of *brega* was no longer audible. We had no oars and no flashlight. A freighter ship could have ploughed us over and sent us to the bottom of the river without ever knowing it had hit us.

Deep in the forest, tree frogs chattered and howler monkeys wailed eerily to each other.

Cézar was thinking about his wife and family; I was thinking of the ten-foot crocodiles.

Then a light loomed out of the darkness, and came quickly up river.

'It's a ship!' cried Cézar in dismay.

It was not a ship, but a motor-powered canoe. Its owner had come to tow us back to the mining town. But it would cost us – 50 *reals*. It was a simple choice: between paying an extortionate figure, or drifting downstream to certain death, and the man knew it. I got out my wallet.

It was almost midnight when we arrived back at Porto Trombetas. Next day I took the boat to Oriximiná, along with the usual rabble of drunken miners. One of them started talking to me, his voice slurred.

'Did you hear about what happened last night at *Vila Paraíso*?'

'No – what?'

'The federal police turned up! They had to hide all the *franguinhas*' – he was using the crude term for young girls. It meant 'little chickens'.

'And only that day they'd brought in some fresh meat ...' he continued. 'Ah well, there's always tomorrow, eh?' He slapped me on the back in a comradely way and staggered back to the bar.

When I arrived in Oriximiná, I visited the town's Children's Council – every town in

Brazil has one. I told the councillors about Bambaloo and the other young girls working in the brothels at *Vila Paraíso*. They were sympathetic. A few months ago they had planned a raid that had to be abandoned when they discovered that the brothel owners already knew about it. The councillors suspected that corrupt police in the town were being paid for information by the brothel owners. A new raid was being planned.

I returned to the quayside just in time to catch my water bus to Manaus, my next destination. The five hundred-mile journey upriver would take three days. This time, I booked a cabin.

12

Manaus: 'Disneylands of Sex'

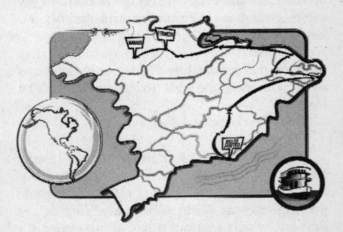

I was glad I had paid for a cabin. It meant I could go to sleep knowing I would not be chewing on somebody's toenails during the night – or that some toothless crone would not be slapping me on the backside, accidentally-on-purpose. I wondered how I had ever managed three days strung up in a hammock. I did feel a few pangs of guilt for being in one of the boat's only six cabins, but they soon passed. The plebeians from 'hammock class' sometimes walked past, gazing covetously as I stretched out luxuriously on my bed or ate my meal. The cabins were always served first; food was brought on a tray, sparing us from the daily scramble at the deck's dinner table.

'You're very courageous, sleeping in a cabin,' on man remarked as I sat on the doorsill of my cabin, eating my rice, beans and *farinha*. 'I'd never be that brave.'

'Pardon?'

'Well, if the boat hits a mud bank and tips over, you won't be able to get out. You'll be trapped.'

'Does that happen a lot?'

'Oh, yes.'

The man went off to join the dinner queue. He was just jealous of my room service and leg-room, I consoled myself. If not, then the people peering into my cabin were marvelling at my bravery, which was not a bad thing either. Or perhaps they were gloating at the foolish for-eigner who would be the first to drown if the boat capsized … I preferred the former.

That night I awoke suddenly to a mighty crash and a violent shudder. Water was pouring through my cabin door. I leaped out of bed and rushed onto the deck, shouting hysterically. A few people peered out of their hammocks and looked at me drowsily. It was just a noisy thunderstorm. The rain was lashing down, the thunder was coming in deafening rolls and sheet lightning was illuminating the sky for several seconds at a time, as if God were flicking the lights on and off. I retired bashfully to my cabin, wondering why my lesson in pride had to be quite so embarrassing.

Manaus was two days away. I took out an envelope sent to me by Amaury Ribeiro, the Brazilian journalist. It contained a series of articles written by Amaury about child prostitution in Manaus for the *O Globo* newspaper in 1997. He and a photographer had gone under cover in some of the casino-bars that lined one of the city-centre streets. There were so many children selling their bodies in the bars that regular visitors had labelled them 'Disneylands of sex'. I'd discussed the articles with Amaury by phone.

'When the story went to press there was a national outcry. The Brazilian president said that he wept when he read it.'

I could see why. Splashed across *O Globo*'s front page was a photograph of a middle-aged man in a shirt and tie, sitting at a table in one of the 'Disneylands'. He was kissing the stomach of a twelve-year-old girl. The bystanders were paying no attention; it was clearly not an unusual sight. The man was a fifty-seven-year-old insurance broker named Benício. 'I've got a woman my own age at home. My business here is *fraguinha* – little chickens. The younger they are, the more excited I get.'

Amaury's article went on to describe how Benício would leave work and make for Tamadaré Street near the docks, armed with a 10-*real* note. It was enough to pick up a girl in one of the 'Disneylands', and book a room in a cheap city-centre hotel.

Another article was an interview with Amazonino Mendes, the state governor of Amazonas, after the 'Disneyland' story broke. He had pledged to crack down on child prostitution in the city, promising to close immediately 'every bar and every place where there is child prostitution in the city'.

But the governor's promises amounted to nothing. 'They did close some of the "Disneylands" immediately after the story was published,' Amaury told me. 'But they opened again as soon as the fuss died down.'

Three days after leaving Oriximiná, the forest began to thin out and the vivid colours started to fade. Instead of tall trees, huge construction cranes towered into the sky, and the thick jungle foliage was replaced by oil refineries pouring out clouds of black smoke. We left the orange and brown waters of the Amazon and joined the jet-black River Negro. The boat chugged slowly toward the docks.

My forehead was drenched in sweat as the bus crawled through Manaus' gridlocked city-centre traffic. The air was heavy and humid, thick with exhaust fumes. I slid the window open and gasped for air. The man sitting next to me chuckled and told me that the people of Manaus sometimes referred to themselves as 'fish', because they breathed in more water than air. I told him that I felt more like a fish in an oil slick.

I got off at the last stop, a busy bus terminal in front of an impressive stone cathedral. From there it was a short distance to Tamandaré Street and the 'Disneylands'.

Tamandaré Street was a cul-de-sac backing on to the docks. It was brimming with boisterous revellers. Men were staggering around swigging from beer bottles, shouting and swearing. *Brega* music blasted out from the casino-bars that lined the street, each competing in decibels with the others. Their names in neon cast coloured patches on the street below: 'Nature', 'Emotions', 'Watercolour', 'Beautiful Art', 'Holland'.

Many of the men on the street were crew members from docked freighter ships and oil tankers. As I walked along the road one man bumped into me, nearly knocking me over. His beer bottle smashed on the ground.

'Hey – idiot!' he bellowed. 'Look what you've done!'

The stocky sailor braced himself for a punch in the face. Instead, I apologised profusely and gave him the money to buy another beer. He took it, completely baffled by my un-sailorlike behaviour.

I dodged other staggering drunks as I walked on down Tamandaré Street. The *Natureza* casino-bar caught my attention – it was one of the 'Disneylands' mentioned in Amaury's report. It was painted with trees and creepers and a snake twisting round a branch. At the entrance stood two burly security guards, arms crossed and muscles bulging. I squeezed past them.

Inside the *Natureza*, a smoke-filled hall was crowded with men, sat around metal tables. The walls were painted with images of *yaporangas*, Amazonian goddesses being swallowed by sea-serpents; there was also a picture of a *boto*, a dolphin turning itself into a man to seduce a young virgin. On a balcony at the far end, a man behind a keyboard sang live *brega* hits, and a girl in a bikini danced energetically. Every wiggle and thrust was met with whoops and cheers, and raucous laughter.

I sat down on an empty table in a far corner of the hall. I watched as women in low-cut dresses or skimpy shorts flirted with groups of men. Most disappeared through a door at the end of the hall. The women were mostly middle-aged, with scrawny legs and sagging bellies, and were plastered in garish make-up. I wondered what diseases were being spread through this establishment.

One of them put a bony hand on my shoulder. 'Hello sailor,' she croaked.

'Ah – I was just leaving,' I stammered, making a dash for the exit.

I had not noticed any young girls in the *Natureza*. However, as I emerged back on to the street I saw a number of girls waiting in front of the casino-bar. One was fifteen-year-old Vanessa. She had curly blond hair, a nose-stud, and an attitude problem.

'I'm not telling you anything. You'll print it in a newspaper and make our lives a misery.'

'I'm not with a newspaper. I just want to hear your story – honestly, I do.'

Vanessa thought for a moment then held out her hand. 'Well – I'm not doing it for nothing. You'll have to pay me.'

I offered to buy her a bag of popcorn, and she agreed to the deal. She sat on the kerbside while I ran over to a popcorn cart on the other side of the road. When I returned Vanessa snatched the bag.

'OK. My whole family died in a plane crash and I became a prostitute. All right?' She got up to leave.

'Hold on! Is that it?'

'What else do you want to know?'

'Well, like … are you happy?'

'My parents and my two brothers are dead. I'm homeless. And I'm selling myself to sailors for 20 *reals* a time. What do you think?'

I conceded that it had been a stupid question. Mollified, Vanessa sat down again. She told me that her family had died a year ago. She was addicted to crack and *mela* – both of them cheap drugs derived from cocaine freebase. She showed me deep scars on her wrists. She had lost count of the times she had tried to kill herself.

'Where do you live?'

'In the Aurora. It's like a hostel.'

'Whereabouts is it?'

'What *is* this? Some kind of interrogation?'

'No – I just ...'

'Right. I'm going.' This time, Vanessa stomped off.

Her friend, fourteen-year-old Jusiane, was more talkative and less wary. She told me that underage girls were not allowed inside the casino-bars any more. So the older women went in and touted on their behalf – taking a cut for themselves, naturally. The taxi drivers were involved in the cover-up. They sometimes took clients straight to the hostels where most of the younger girls stayed, out of sight.

'*Younger* girls?' I asked.

'Oh yeah. There are some ten-year-old girls living in the hostels. But they're not allowed out.'

'Jusiane, would you take me to the hostels?'

She laughed. 'Are you kidding? The owner would kill us both!'

A while later I saw Vanessa meet a man as he left the *Natureza*. They got into a taxi. I hailed another. 'Follow that taxi!'

We drove past the dock gates and the cathedral square, then down a deserted road lined with warehouses. Finally we turned into a small, dimly-lit road called Joaquim Nabuco. There were a number of shabby hostels called 'hotels' and 'guesthouses', with hinged signs and wooden shutters.

Vanessa's taxi stopped in front of the Aurora Hotel. I watched as the two got out and pushed hurriedly through a narrow wooden door at the side of the hostel.

I instructed the driver to wait for me, got out of the taxi and crossed the road towards the Aurora. The road was shadowy and eerily quiet. I pushed open the door and peered cautiously inside. There was a narrow alleyway that disappeared into the shadows. A huge rat scurried out of the darkness and ran over my foot. My heart raced.

Stepping inside, I let the door go slowly and ventured a few metres into the alleyway. It smelt damp and foul. In the silence, I could hear footsteps above me and faint high-pitched shouts and giggles from somewhere that echoed in the darkness. I walked a few steps further, unable to see much more than my hand in front of me.

Suddenly I could hear heavy breathing close to me. Then I was face-to-face with a burly man with a hairy face and bulging eyes. I froze.

'What do you want?' growled a deep, menacing voice.

Words would not come. I stepped backwards, tripping over myself. It seemed like an age before I stumbled onto the door, pushed it open and lurched back onto the road.

I looked over the road for my taxi-driver, but he had gone. The road was deserted. As instinct took over I began to run in the direction we had come, losing myself in the identical-looking roads of warehouses and loading bays.

I eventually found my way back to the main road that led back to the cathedral square. I walked back towards the bus terminal.

Three girls were sitting on the ledge of a shop window, shuttered with a metal roller-blind. They were huddled together, their T-shirts stretched across their knees, sniffing bags of glue.

'Whoaaaaaa! Who are you?' one shouted in alarm as I approached.

'It's all right. I just want to talk.'

The girls stopped sniffing and scrutinised me warily. I introduced myself. Before long they were chatting excitedly, each competing with the others to be heard. Micaeli, a thirteen-year-old with frizzy black hair, was the leader. Vera Lúcia had short, cropped hair; she was also thirteen. Twelve-year-old Waldinéia was the youngest and the smallest. Her mother was from the Indian *Yanomami* tribe, and Waldinéia had inherited her features. The other girls called her 'Little Indian'.

Micaeli did most of the talking.

'I don't know why I came on to the streets,' she admitted. 'I used to come shopping with my mother in the city centre. I'd see the street girls and think, "I want to be like that." Stupid, really.'

'I know why I'm here,' said Vera, still hiding her face under her T-shirt. 'My family doesn't care about me. They never treated me very well. Whenever I – '

'Oh, my mum cares about me all right,' interrupted Micaeli. 'When I go home she cries and begs me to come home. That's why I don't go home very often,' she explained.

A yellow taxi screeched to a halt in front of us.

'Wanna earn some money?'

The driver was brash and confident. He leaned out of his cab window and made a very suggestive gesture to the girls. 'How about it, then? All three?'

I was shocked – the girls were so young, and had such a child-like manner.

'F— off!' Micaeli shouted. The taxi-driver returned her expletive with one of his own, then sped off in a crunch of gears. I looked at the girls with a new respect.

'Well, we've got to be careful,' said Micaeli defensively. 'A friend of mine went off with a taxi driver and she never came back. That's why I never get in a car with a man.'

They sold their bodies on street corners, the girls told me, or waited outside the 'Disneylands' on Tamandaré Street. They spent the money on food and clothes.

'What are we supposed to do?' demanded Waldinéia. 'No-one gives us anything for nothing. They always want something in return.'

I asked how much they charged.

'Ten *reals*,' said Micaeli decisively. Then she hesitated and pondered for a moment. 'I won't lie to you. Sometimes I do it for five. But never less than five!' she insisted. 'Well, unless I really need the money ...'

'But you're all so young,' I said.

'Young? I'm thirteen years old!' replied Vera Lúcia. 'Most of the girls are *much* younger than me.'

The girls had spotted my digital camera and soon discovered that it could shoot short movie clips, and that they could watch the clips on the camera. They giggled and squirmed in delight as they took turns talking to the camera, then crowded round to watch the playback.

'Hello!' sniggered a bashful Vera Lúcia, staring alluringly into the lens. 'My name's Vera, I'm thirteen years old. I want to marry – let me see – oh, someone rich and handsome –'

'My turn!' squealed Waldinéia, pushing Vera aside. 'My name's Waldinéia. I'm twelve, and I –'

A sudden giggling fit overcame her and she was too embarrassed to continue. She hid her head in her T-shirt and retired in some confusion.

'It's my turn now,' said Micaeli. 'Come on, shut up. I'm going to say something serious.'

The others stopped giggling. Micaeli combed her hair back with her fingers from her deep, expressive eyes, revealing three scratches on her cheek.

'My name's Micaeli, I'm thirteen. My dream is to have my own things, and to be able to arrange them neatly on my own table in my own room. And my other dream is to dance on the platform in the church. Thank you.' She blew a kiss to the camera.

'Well, that's my dream *as well*,' said Vera Lúcia.

They walked down the street with me, still chatting and playing around, and all the taking deep breaths from their bags of glue. We reached the cathedral. They said goodbye and jumped on to the back of a rubbish truck.

'Glue-sniffers!' shouted the driver of a black sports car as he drove past.

'Glue sniffer's your mother!' Micaeli shouted back, to the great approval of the other two.

I walked back to the bus terminal and sat down on a concrete bench.

The midnight chimes of the cathedral clock floated out over the hot and sticky air. Behind me the 'Disneylands' were gearing up for the night: *brega* music was thumping out the usual tiresome beat. Another group of girls crossed the road ahead of me, heading towards Tamandaré Street. They walked in high heels and wore heavy make-up, but underneath they were so obviously just children. Tears came unbidden to my eyes.

Then I broke down and buried my head in my hands, sobbing bitterly. The handful of people waiting for the last bus glanced uneasily at me. Suddenly I felt completely overwhelmed, completely helpless. I had been travelling this vast country for more than four months. But for the first time I could not cope with what I was seeing.

I will always remember that moment. More than any other time on my journey, I felt God's inconsolable heartbreak, his unquenchable anger, and his limitless love as he looked upon his world – and what was being done to his children.

'I need to get to Bolivia! How far can you take me?' I shouted across to the skipper of the *Almirante Moreira*. It carried a sign showing that it would be sailing up the Madeira River, whose source is in the Bolivian Andes.

'Just up to Porto Velho,' the bearded captain shouted back. 'The boats can only go that far, because of the waterfalls. You'll have to carry on by land.'

'Got any cabins?'

'Yeah – *en suite*, too. I'll do you a good price.'

'What about the mud banks?' I was beginning to be familiar with Brazilian river travel.

'No problem! I'll steer clear of them!'

'How long to Porto Velho?'

'Four days.'

I handed over my money and the captain scrawled a ticket on a piece of paper and passed it down to me.

The last leg of my trip would take me to Guajará-Mirim, a town on the Bolivian border. I had heard about the town from Graça Prola, co-ordinator of the *Estação-Direito* foundation in Manaus. I had gone to see her to ask her about the child prostitution problem in Manaus, but she had told me something else; that Brazilian girls were being smuggled over the border to Bolivia.

Brazil is a vast country, and it had been easy to imagine so far that the problems I had been witnessing were confined to its boundaries. Graça's information now showed that the Brazilian child abuse industry was not limited to Brazil but reached out to its neighbours. I knew of the Italian cartels and the European brothels that took on children considered too old to be profitable any more in Brazil. But this was different, and I knew it was different, as I listened to Graça's account of boats crossing the river, ferrying the young prostitutes over the Bolivian border. The next stage of the journey, I decided, had to be Bolivia.

That afternoon, I phoned Amaury at the *Isto É* newsroom in Brasília. I had promised to let him know what I had found out about the 'Disneylands' – he had been eager to know if his article had had any lasting effect. During our conversation I mentioned what Graça Prola had told me, and my decision to go to the border.

'Sounds like a story,' he said. 'When will you get there?'

'I'm leaving tonight. I'll probably get to Guajará-Mirim on Tuesday evening.'

'I'll meet you there,' he said decisively. 'It will be a good story for *Isto É*. We can research it together.'

I was glad that he would be coming along. The story was becoming very big, and very dark.

13

Guajará-Mirim: 'Nobody can rescue me from this'

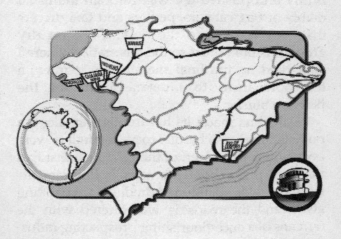

I leaned over the deck rail and watched the unchanging landscape. The *Almirante Moreira* was making slow progress along the Madeira River, patiently following its huge meandering curves that twisted like a thin snake through the dense virgin rainforest. The water was an impenetrable muddy brown. Bubbles rose constantly to the surface and burst, as if the boat were navigating a simmering cauldron of melting chocolate.

Eventually the boat came to a halt in the gurgling, bubbling waters outside Porto Velho, capital of the remote Brazilian state of Rondônia. A precarious gangplank was pushed out to the bank, and soon a stream of passengers was wobbling to the shore. I gripped my bags firmly and pushed my way through the usual rabble of bag carriers, pedlers and taxi drivers that had leapt onto the deck. Once on dry ground, I took a taxi to the bus station where I embarked on the final stage of my journey; a four-hour ride to Guajará-Mirim on the Bolivian border.

As the bus made its hazardous way along a potholed and treacherous road, reminders were everywhere to be seen of the gold rush that had made the region briefly famous. In tiny tributaries of the river, abandoned dredgers were rotting away, and the roadside was littered with the remains of a once-flourishing prospecting industry. After the first hour or so, I began to see for the first time the devastation that is happening to the Brazilian rainforests: immense areas cut down, and desolate tracts of land, once green and fertile and now burnt black and desolate.

Amaury was waiting at the bus station in Guajará-Mirim. He had arrived that morning

by plane from the *Isto É* magazine office in
Brasília, and had been looking round.

'Are you sure there's something going on
here?' he asked, as I waited to collect my
luggage from the bus. 'The place seems
completely deserted.' He seemed a little disappointed. I wondered uneasily whether I might
have lured the celebrated journalist into the
middle of nowhere for nothing.

He could be right, I thought, as we walked
through the town centre streets. Most of the
shops were boarded up, and the roads were
eerily quiet. The few people sauntering in the
streets only made it seem more like a ghost
town, an impression made all the stronger by
the rusting steam locomotive, eternally motionless on rusted tracks, standing outside the
derelict train station.

Guajará-Mirim was the last town in Brazil.
The half-mile-wide, choppy waters of the
Mamoré River separated the town from the
Bolivian town of Guayaramerin. At the ferry
terminal a few small passenger boats waited
hopefully for business.

There were only a handful of hotels in
Guajará-Mirim. None had any guests. The
receptionist at the *Jamaica* looked bored and
unimpressed by our arrival. The limping, mut-
tering porter who showed us to our rooms
seemed to have lost interest in his job a long
time ago.

Our only contact in Guajará-Mirim was Izabel Hayden, the voluntary president of the town's Children's Council. Graça Prola in Manaus had given me her telephone number when she had told me about the traffic of young Brazilian girls to Bolivia. When we had done our unpacking we decided to ring Izabel.

Amaury dialled her number. I sat on my bed listening to half of a conversation that began with an explanation of who we were and why we were in town, and grew increasingly animated.

'Yes … right … Of course, no! … Yes, sure … OK, *tchau*.' He put the phone down.

'So?' I asked, impatiently.

'She says she can't talk on the phone, it's too risky. And she said she's got something very important to tell us. And she wants us to go and see her tomorrow.'

I lay back on the bed, apprehensive but satisfied that at least the journey had not been for nothing. Tomorrow we were obviously going to learn something worth coming to Guajará-Mirim for.

'And she said that under *no* circumstances were we to cross the border to Bolivia – before speaking to her.'

'Yeah?'

'She said we could get into very serious trouble if we did.'

He put his shoes on and starting tying his laces. I didn't need to ask what was going through

Amaury's mind. I knew enough of his reputation as one of Brazil's best investigative journalists to be sure that he wasn't planning an early night. If Izabel had wanted to stop him going to Bolivia, she had said exactly the wrong thing.

I reached for my own shoes and put them on.

We waited until nightfall before making the crossing into Bolivia. There were no border formalities; we would not need passports unless we planned to go further into Bolivia.

At the river we boarded one of the many small boats plying for trade. The current we were crossing was strong, and the boat strained to keep itself from being dragged downstream. The noises of its small engine were mixed with the groaning of protesting metal as we inched our way on to the pebbly shore at Guayaramerin.

The Bolivian town could hardly have been more different to its similarly-named Brazilian neighbour. Its streets were lively and bustling; as we disembarked, men in tattered suits waved wads of dollars at us from wooden desks, shouting exchange rates at the tops of their voices. This illegal *bureau de change* was a way of laundering money made from the drugs trade: the small town was one of the main smuggling routes into Brazil.

The road from the ferry was buzzing with mopeds and motor cycles. Motorbike rickshaws

stood in line, each with a brightly painted passenger carriage. As we headed for town the
young drivers ran after us, calling volubly to us
in Spanish. Amaury took one of them aside.

'Listen, *amigo*. You must know what goes on
here. I need your help with something.'

'*Si Señor*,' he replied. 'Here we say, *Tienes
dinero, tienes todo!*' I recognised the words from
their Portuguese equivalent. 'Have money,
have everything.'

Amaury produced a 10-*real* note from his
wallet. The driver seized it, carried it to a streetlight to inspect it and, satisfied, stuffed it into
his pocket.

'OK. I know a good place. Quality stuff. How
many kilos do you want?'

'Kilos? No – you don't understand! We don't
want drugs.'

Amaury launched into *espunhol*, a patois of
Portuguese and broken Spanish. We were looking
for young girls, he said – specifically, Brazilian
young girls. The driver nodded vigorously. He
could take us to *La Magnifica*, he suggested, a
brothel specialising in what we wanted. It was in
Riberalta province, two hours from Guayaramerin. It would cost an extra 30 *reals*, 80
bolivianos. Amaury took out his wallet again.

We clutched the metal frame of the rickshaw
as it hurtled out of town, its engine roaring. The
narrow dirt roads threw up clouds of dust and
the vehicle threatened to overturn as we

lurched from side to side. Eventually we arrived at a clearing where a pink neon sign displayed a garish image of Eve biting an apple and the words, *La Magnifica*. The driver said he would wait for us.

The saloon was ugly and and oppressive, its black walls painted with luminous green and black Aztec patterns. Flickering candles hung from the ceiling. Loudspeakers were grinding out the strumming of Spanish guitars. At the bar, a woman was wiping glasses.

'Are you open?'

She looked at Amaury blankly. He tried again. *'Estas abierto?'*

'Si! Si . . . perdonome.' She scurried round the bar and showed us to a table. Amaury asked if there were any Brazilian girls.

'Brasileñas? Si, si. Um momento, por favor.'

Moments later a nervous brunette appeared from behind a bead curtain and sat down with us. She smiled when we greeted her in Portuguese. Her name was Samara and she was from Várzea Grande, a town in the Brazilian state of Mato Grosso.

'I haven't been to Brazil for six months – not since I turned sixteen and came to work here. I ran away from home when I was twelve. My mum's boyfriend used to beat me up – I couldn't take it any more. So I got a lift with a truck driver going north.'

When she arrived in Rio Branco, a city near the Bolivian border, she was still wearing her school uniform. A taxi driver made Samara an offer she could not refuse. That same day she sold her virginity to a drugs baron in Guayaramerin for $150. 'That's how I started. They paid me in dollars and I got free drugs.'

She drained a tequila. Four years after leaving her violent stepfather, the pretty sixteen-year-old was addicted to cocaine and alcohol. Now she was not even paid in *bolivianos*, let alone dollars. Now she sold her body for a room in a brothel and a supply of drugs and drink.

'I still miss my mum and little sisters. But I probably won't ever see them again. I expect they think I'm dead.'

Over at the bar, the woman was growing suspicious, glancing at us with open hostility as our conversation continued with no sign of money changing hands. I began to be worried, remembering Izabel's warning to Amaury. Had we been incredibly stupid? If anything happened to us here, nobody would ever know … I heaved a large inward sigh of relief when Amaury suggested we should leave. We said goodbye and left, followed by curious and unfriendly glances. The rickshaw driver too seemed suspicious at our hasty departure.

'You didn't like *La Magnifica*?' he shouted over his shoulder, as we roared along the road to Guayaramerin.

'Pardon?' Amaury shouted back.

'Well! You didn't stay for any of the girls …'

Amaury improvised. 'Too old! We were looking for younger girls. *Compreendes?'*

'Really? You won't find them here. Not unless you're a *barão* or as businessman.'

'Why's that?'

The driver explained that Brazilian girls younger than sixteen came to Bolivia only for the *barões* – the town's drug barons. He was always picking up girls from the passenger boats, he assured us, and taking them to the mansions. 'The little girls belong to the barons. Nobody else.'

'Can we see where the barons live? Will you take us there?'

He flatly refused. 'There's no way I'd do a thing like that. I could end up dead if I did.'

We had missed the last passenger boat to Brazil by the time we got to the ferry terminal in Guayaramerin. We had to hire a motor-powered canoe to make the return crossing over the Mamoré, arriving back in our hotel in the early hours.

'You did *what*?'

Izabel Hayden leaned across her desk in her small office in Guajará-Mirim's town hall, and stared at us in disbelief.

'You're crazy, both of you. Didn't I warn you last night?'

She calmed down as quickly as she had erupted. Her voice softened somewhat into the quiet speech that seemed to be her normal style of conversation. 'If anybody had suspected anything, they would have killed you in cold blood. I mean it.'

She glanced across at the door of her office. She had carefully closed it tight when we came in. The office had flimsy walls, obviously partitioning what had once been a much larger office, and she now lowered her voice as if afraid that the people we could hear talking in neighbouring offices might overhear.

'It's a very, very big business. Prostitution of Brazilian girls in Bolivia is run by the drug barons in Guayaramerin. They're linked with the Cali Cartel. You know who they are?'

We both needed no explanation: the cartel was one of the biggest drug rings in South America.

Izabel sat back in her chair and gestured expressively. 'What can I tell you? The barons have go-betweens who recruit poor girls in Guajará-Mirim. They hang around school gates, or approach the girls in discos. At first they give them designer clothes and mobile phones. It's like entering a different world for those girls.'

Izabel knew of over three hundred girls involved in the Bolivian prostitution ring. None was over fifteen years old, and some were as young as eight. Every day they made the crossing on the passenger boats to Guayaramerin, where the rickshaw drivers collected them and took them to the mansions of the drugs barons.

'The barons organise big parties at their mansions where the girls are available. They can earn $200 a night when they start. They get free drugs, like cannabis and cocaine. But once they're addicted, their price starts to drop – and the older a girl is, the less she earns.'

She told us more about the reason why we had seen no girls under sixteen in the Bolivian brothel.

'The barons have a rule: girls under sixteen are their property, no one else can have them. And once they're sixteen the drugs barons don't want them any more. They're "used goods", that's what they say.'

By that age most were addicted to hard drugs. They were sent to run-down Bolivian brothels like *La Magnifica*, where they sold their bodies not for money but for a fix of drugs or a measure of alcohol.

'Some of the prettiest are sold to brothels in Europe – for huge sums of money. They end up as sex slaves in places like Spain or Portugal.'

She knew of at least sixty girls who had gone to Campo Grande, a town in the state of Mato Grosso. It was almost a certainty that a girl going to Mato Grosso would in due course be trafficked to Europe – 'Campo Grande is a kind of training camp,' said Izabel. 'None of the girls who go there ever come back. And their families never hear from them again.'

Many of the girls had confided in Izabel. She told us of an eight-year-old already addicted to cocaine. At least eight girls had contracted HIV. One, a fifteen-year-old, had tried to escape. She had been found in the river with a bullet hole in her forehead.

'Another girl begged me to help her to escape,' Izabel told me. 'She told me, "They want to send me to the house in Campo Grande." I managed to get her out, but her whole family had to move to another part of the country. From then on I started getting death threats. One man rang me at home, at night. He told me to leave the girls alone or – then, next day, I was going to work on my moped and a car with blacked-out windows came up alongside me. It deliberately knocked me off the road. I was really shaken up.'

When Izabel's family, who lived in São Luis – a coastal city near Fortaleza, almost a thousand miles away – also began to receive threats, Izabel decided that enough was enough. 'That's when I decided to back off. There are a lot of powerful people involved. And that's why you should be careful, too.'

I was busy taking notes but my mind was trying to come to grips with what Izabel was saying. The story had shifted alarmingly away from the conversations I had had with young girls in sunlit town squares, or visiting their homes and even their workplaces. Now it had become a story of an enclave of immensely rich, powerful men to whom the life of a human being apparently meant very little – whether that life belonged to a little girl sold into drugs and prostitution, or to a British journalist who stuck his nose into their business a little too far. My imagination was painting all sorts of pictures and devising numerous scenarios, all ending horribly. I knew that if things went wrong, we could easily end up shot or stabbed. Ours would certainly not be the first corpses to be dumped into the convenient waters of the Mamoré River.

The room seemed suddenly chilly. I shivered, and tried to think of other things. 'Who does the actual recruiting here in Guajará-Mirim?'

Izabel glanced again at the door. 'Give me your notepad,' she said. I passed it across the desk. She took a pen and wrote, in neat, deliberate letters, the name *Elias Quintão*. 'That's the most dangerous of the lot. He's gay, a hairdresser. He's very persuasive. He tells the girls that he wants to take them to Bolivia to appear in fashion shows.'

'How do we find him?' asked Amaury.

'He's always at the *Planeta* club on Friday nights. That's where he makes contact with the girls. But you're not going to try to talk to him, are you? *Are* you?'

We arranged to meet up with her again, later in the week.

Girls got into the *Planeta* free before midnight.
The boys queued impatiently outside, filing
through the nightclub's turnstile and paying
their five *reals*. Amaury and I were among
them.

Inside, ear-splitting dance music throbbed
and coloured lights flickered on and off, bursts
of strobe lighting up the teenagers packed on to
the dance floor.

It was almost midnight when Elias arrived.
He made quite an entrance, accompanied by an
entourage of men all dressed similarly to
himself: asphyxiatingly tight trousers and a
glittering top that exposed his midriff. They all
danced together in the centre of the floor:
absorbed in their movements, flinging their
arms flamboyantly into the air to the beat.
Amaury and I danced over towards them. I
tried to forget that I was almost face to face with
one of the most dangerous men in the region, a
man who would have me killed as easily as
look at me; but it was hard work.

'How are we going to speak to him?' Amaury
shouted into my ear. "And how are we going to
take his picture without him noticing?"

I had an idea. 'Hold on,' I shouted back, and
shuffled up to where the group was dancing.
Forgetting all my inhibitions, I twisted my arms
above my head and wiggled my bottom, gyrat-
ing around the outside of Elias' circle. Across
the dance floor, Amaury was dealing with an

attack of hysterical giggles. It was not long before Elias spotted me.

'Hey, come into our circle!' he shouted.

I was unlikely to bump into anyone I knew in a disco on the Bolivian border, I told myself, and joined Elias, continuing my ridiculous dance. As the strobes started flashing again I got my camera out and discreetly took some close-ups of Elias. He did not notice.

'Nice moves,' he bellowed. 'Where you from?'

'England!' I swivelled round on my heels.

'What are you doing here?'

I told him the cover story we'd concocted. We were travel agents, I said, and were in town looking for young girls for our rich clients. His eyes lit up.

'I think I can help you. Let's go outside and talk.'

I called Amaury, and we went outside together. I switched on my tape recorder surreptitiously as we went – if we were going to publish Elias' name in the magazine, we needed solid evidence to back it up. I was beginning to develop a kind of desperado mentality. We were in too deep to back out now. I tried to forget what would happen if Elias noticed the microphone.

'I know plenty of young girls,' Elias bragged. 'All of them under fifteen. I can get you as many as you want, as young as you want. Just let me know.'

We asked him where we could meet his girls.

'You'll have to meet them on the Bolivian side, sure – that's the safest way. Nobody will bother you there.'

He passed me a scrap of paper with his address and mobile phone number, then turned on his heel and went back inside the *Planeta*.

We had all the evidence we needed. My heart didn't stop thumping until we were nearly back at the hotel.

As we arrived in the foyer, Amaury was still laughing about my dancing. 'If you don't put that in your book, I'll write an article about it in the magazine!'

Back in our room, our adrenaline drained away. Amaury was no longer laughing. Our conversation was interrupted by long pauses, as we relived the evening's escapade. Delayed reaction was setting in.

'That was a very dangerous man,' acknowledged Amaury. 'Whooh! Maybe we should have listened to Izabel after all.'

Neither of us believed that. But we realised that we had sailed very close to the wind, and having told no-one where we were going, we would have vanished without trace if things had gone wrong.

'What do we do next?'

Amaury answered immediately. 'We go home. We've got the evidence and people across the river are starting to notice us. It might not be so easy to get out a few days from now.'

I agreed. I needed no persuading.

Next morning we packed and paid our hotel bill. But before setting off back to Porto Velho, we remembered our promise to call at Izabel's house.

'Thank goodness you're here,' she greeted us. 'I've been trying to reach you all morning.'

She had managed to make contact with one of the girls involved in the prostitution ring in Guayaramerin. The girl had been selling her body to the Bolivian drugs barons since she was eleven. She was now sixteen.

'She says she's too afraid to talk to you in person, but she'll talk to you on the phone provided I don't tell you her name.'

The voice on the phone was distant and shaky. She was obviously very frightened. I asked her how she had become involved with the Bolivian ring.

'I was young, I didn't know what I was getting into. I needed the money. I didn't think it would get so serious.'

She sometimes had sex with clients more than ten times in a night. At twelve she had become addicted to cocaine. Now she spent all her earnings on drugs. Soon she would be sixteen and the drugs barons would not want her any more.

'They want to send me to Europe,' she said, her voice trembling. 'I don't know what to do. If I don't go ...'

'Why don't you try to get out? I'm sure Izabel will help you.'

'If I did that,' said the faint voice at the other end of the line, 'they'd come after me and kill me. No, I don't think anybody can rescue me from this.' She began to cry. I passed the phone back to Izabel.

A few weeks after the phone conversation the girl disappeared. Nothing has been heard from her since.

At Porto Velho, Amaury and I said goodbye at the airport. His next assignment was to cover a breaking corruption scandal about one of the candidates for the forthcoming presidential elections. We promised to keep in touch.

His article appeared in *Isto É* magazine a month later as the front cover story: 'Girls – Export Product'. It shook Brazilian society. In five pages Amaury exposed the traffic of Brazilian girls into Bolivia and on into Europe.

The story was advertised on tens of thousands of billboards all over Brazil, and was carried on national TV. As a result of its publication a number of those named in the article were arrested, and a federal investigation was set up. The publicity arising from the exposure led to an agreement being signed between Brazil and Bolivia to police the border – an undertaking that cost millions of dollars.

It was a hugely satisfying result for an adventure that had been physically dangerous and emotionally harrowing.

'The bus to Rio de Janeiro is now boarding on Platform 6.'

I shuffled impatiently down the queue to buy my ticket for the two thousand-mile journey back to Rio.

Over the three days of the trip Brazil showed herself to me in all her rich variety of landscape and scenery, as if I were retracing the journey I'd been making since leaving Copacabana Beach, so long, it seemed, ago.

We drove for hours through the rainforest, Brazil's fast-depleting, magnificent treasure, still one of the great wonders of the world despite the appalling damage being done to it every day. The forest eventually gave way to green rolling hills, typical of ones I'd driven through on my journey.

The road next passed through a region of well-cultivated properties, densely planted and obviously fertile, a reminder of the natural resources with which Brazil has been blessed. That too eventually gave way, to the brick-red soil of the scrub land as we approached Rio. This time I was in one of the big vehicles, looking down on the termite mounds, the tumbleweed and the occasional small car like that in which I'd begun my trip.

And then the familiar skyline of Rio was in view, and the embracing arms of the statue of Christ on the hilltop, and the sea and the airport beyond.

I was going home.

Postscript: Islington, London

An icy wind blows against my face, leaving me breathless. My breath escapes in clouds of mist; my hands are numb with cold.

Brazil seems far away now. That country of bizarre contrasts – struggling between prosperity and suffering, culture and barbarity, lush green forests and spoiled black wasteland – is thousands of miles distant. Were I to board a plane right now, it would be half a day before I landed in Rio.

Now everything is back to normal, whatever 'normal' means. I pass fashionable restaurants, bars and familiar high street stores. Upper Street is a stream of faces, pouring out of the Underground station or emerging from London's bright red double-decker buses.

I am now working for the Daily Mirror newspaper, having done my deferred postgraduate course in journalism. I live and work in a world of paved streets, large superstores, grand buildings, trim parks: the only river I see now is the comfortable slow-moving Thames, its murky waters lapping the Houses of Parliament, the Embankment and dozens of other places I know by heart. If I tried very hard I might even be able to think Brazil away like a dream, as I negotiate the concrete and tar-mac of modern London; as I chase stories and try to meet deadlines. I am back: I am home.

Yet in a thousand different ways I am not. Nothing is quite as it was before. Those six months in Brazil have changed me for ever.

As I fight my way through London's chaotic rush-hour crowd, I scan the faces and furrowed brows. They reflect the rich multicultural diver-sity of the capital; skin tones ranging from ebony black to pale Caucasian, neat suits and flamboyant African head scarves, blonde Madonna wannabees and sleekly styled black hair – if I don't look too hard, some of those faces I see might almost be those of the children I have left behind.

The frightened girl on the end of a crackling phone line on the Bolivian border; Micaeli, Vera Lúcia and Waldinéia, giggling and playing on a street corner in Manaus; fragile Fabíola from Santarém, her eyes betraying the painful mem-ories that just won't go away; the children from the Bat's Hole in Belém; Michele, waiting awk-wardly on Fortaleza's 'whores' point'; playful

Romilda in Recife; the gang of '1.99 girls' in Governador Valadares; pretty Sabrina, her virginity sold to the highest bidder; and the little, frightened girl cowering on the beach at Copacabana. I never did find her again, and I never discovered her name.

A warm blast strikes my face as I enter the Underground station. I push through the crowds and take my place on a steep escalator. The faces of London rise and pass me as I descend; each of them an individual, each with their own plans for the day, each infinitely precious to God.

Tears well up in my eyes; I am back in Brazil. I can still see each of the children. I can hear their voices: some imploring, some desperate to be rescued: most simply wanting to be remembered.

And I won't – can't – forget them, however hard I try. Those few girls passed only fleetingly through my life, but they left an indelible impression. Even six months on, the memory of them is still difficult to cope with, and I am still struggling to find an adequate response.

But what I saw in Brazil was just a tiny fraction of what God sees every minute of the day. He is all-knowing, all-seeing. He cannot turn away, he cannot cover his eyes or ears. I know that I will never fully understand God's heart, or truly grasp just how much God loves the poor and suffering, the victims of injustice.

God knows where the little girl from Copacabana is. Whatever is happening to her, whatever abuse, whatever violence, God sees it. Whatever she is feeling, God is feeling it too.

He knows what happens behind closed doors and in the darkness of the night. He feels every hurt, hears every desperate cry. Only when we realise this do we begin to understand God's beating heart, what he loves and what he hates. God sees, and he is absolutely outraged, absolutely furious, absolutely indignant.

'Administer justice every morning,' he cries to his people. 'Rescue from the hand of his oppressor the one who has been robbed, or my wrath will break out and burn like fire ... with no-one to quench it.' (Jeremiah 21:12)

This truth is still sinking in. But I know it will have – must have – major consequences for the way I live my life.

Of course, my journey around Brazil achieved results. Some were small successes, like Fabíola and her baby, now being cared for in a safe, loving environment. Some were more far-reaching, like Amaury's article, the repercussions of which are still being felt today. And there are other results still being developed. One of those projects is described at the end of this book.

The train slows down and the lights of the station pour through the windows. I look around the crowded carriage. Crammed into its narrow space is a sampling of all the countries of the world. Each traveller is a unique person, coming from somewhere and heading for somewhere else; each one of them a story that could fill a book.

Imagine what would happen if we looked at the world the way God does; if we shared his outrage and indignation, his compassion for the victims of injustice, the vulnerable, the forgotten. Imagine if we really loved others in the way God does, without restrictions, without prejudices. Imagine if we took seriously his command to do justice every morning, to 'rescue from the hands of the oppressor the one who has been robbed'. In Brazil, in Africa, in Palestine, in Iraq, in our country, in our own communities ...

... We would turn the world upside down.

The Next Chapter: Pedraviva

The next chapter of this book hasn't yet been written, but with your help it could be filled with hope.

When I returned from Brazil I set up a charity in the UK to support projects working with some of Brazil's most vulnerable children, like the ones I had met on my journey. The first project we are supporting was started by a close friend of mine called Nilce from Belo Horizonte. Let me explain. . .

Nilce is the headteacher of one of Belo Horizonte's biggest state schools, situated just metres away from one of Belo's biggest and most violent slums, *Pedreira* – meaning 'The Quarry'. *Pedreira* is notorious for drug-dealing and gang warfare, and many of the young girls are involved in prostitution.

When she took over as headteacher three years ago, Nilce started an after-school project teaching dance and music to some of her most difficult students. She later introduced other workshops, such as carpet-making and tapestry. The project became an enormous success, helping many of the teenagers to tackle their problems and overcome their addictions.

We now want to extend the project to other schools in every one of Belo Horizonte's slums. The after-school club is now a registered Brazilian charity, called *Pedraviva*. This name, which means 'Living Stones', is after the teenagers of The Quarry who have found a new direction for their lives against overwhelming odds. We now have our own office and many willing volunteers, including the young people whom the project first helped.

Pedraviva is such an innovative and exciting project, and one that is very close to my heart. I really believe we could touch the lives of many thousands of boys and girls struggling to grow up in a culture where violence and abuse are tragically commonplace. I want to invite you to get involved in making *Pedraviva* a real success. With your help we can write a happy ending to this book.

There are many ways you can help, from giving to praying to going. Please get in touch if you would like to get involved, or visit www.mattroper.com.

You can e-mail me at: mattroper@terra.com.br

Or write to:

Pedraviva
La Corbiere
Caudwell Drive
Mansfield
Notts
NG18 4SL

www.mattroper.com

Remember Me, Rescue Me is an interactive book. By logging on to **www.mattroper.com** you can see pictures of Matt's journey around Brazil chapter by chapter, including photos of the places and people in this book. You can also post your own message to other readers and write your own review. Most importantly, you can find out what you can do to help girls caught up in Brazil's sex industry.